The Illustrated Buyer's Guide to
Oriental Carpets

Schiffer Publishing

J.R. Azizollahoff

4880 Lower Valley Rd. Atglen, PA 19310 USA

In Memory of Menashe Azizollahoff

About the Values

Estimates of value are the opinion of the author and are approximations of current retail prices as of April 1997. Neither publisher nor author assumes any liability for variances in the pricing or dating of any carpet illustrated herein. Numerous rugs illustrated herein are copyrighted and/or trademarked by their creators or owners and may not be reproduced without their express written consent.

Library of Congress Cataloging-in-Publication Data

Azizollahoff, J.R.
    The illustrated buyer's guide to Oriental carpets / J.R. Azizollahoff.
        p. cm.
    Includes bibliographical references and index.
    ISBN 0-7643-0436-4 (hc)
    1. Rugs, Oriental.   I. Title.
NK2808.A94   1998
746.7'5'095--dc21   97-44388
                                                     CIP

Designed by Bonnie M. Hensley

ISBN: 0-7643-0436-4
Printed in Hong Kong
1 2 3 4

Published by Schiffer Publishing Ltd.
4880 Lower Valley Road
Atglen, PA 19310
Phone: (610) 593-1777; Fax: (610) 593-2002
E-mail: Schifferbk@aol.com
Please write for a free catalog.
This book may be purchased from the publisher.
Please include $3.95 for shipping.

Please try your bookstore first.

We are interested in hearing from authors
with book ideas on related subjects.

Acknowledgements

I wish to thank my wife, Li Kwang, for her love and support, and my late uncle, Eli Azizollahoff, for teaching me and a generation of old carpet wholesalers how to value rugs.

I am grateful to Barry Kamali of Kamali Oriental Rugs, New York, for his generous donation of many old rug transparencies, and Professor Henry Glassie, for writing the foreword. Also, I am indebted to the following donors of transparencies who are members of the Oriental Rug Importers Association in New York City: Eliko Antique and Decorative Rugs, Harounian Rugs International Co., Hasid Oriental Rugs, Inc., Michaelian and Kohlberg, Inc., Abraham Moheban & Son, Odegard, Inc., Pande Cameron & Co., Inc., and Renaissance Carpet & Tapestries, Inc. In addition, I am beholden to the following contributors of transparencies who are members of the Oriental Rug Importers Association in Secaucus, New Jersey: Aminco, Inc., Fazeli/Trans Orient, Inc., Global Rug Corp./Woven Arts, Inc., Lotfy & Sons, Inc., Noonoo Rug Co., Inc., Samad Brothers, Inc., and Soleimani Rug Co. Also, I must convey my gratitude to the following supporters of this undertaking who readily bestowed transparencies: Alice's Antiques, New York City, John Batki, Syracuse, New York, N. Ben Chafieian Oriental Rugs, New York City, Christie's, Inc., New York City, Couristan, Inc., Fort Lee, New Jersey, Louis De Poortere, Adairsville, Georgia, French Accents Rugs & Tapestries, Inc., New York City, Iraj Fine Oriental Rugs, Inc., New York City, Karastan, Calhoun, Georgia, Marian B. Miller, New York City, Nourison Rug Corp., Saddle Brook, New Jersey, Peel & Company, Inc., Mandeville, Louisiana, Rahmanan Oriental Rugs, New York City, Woven Legends, Inc., Philadelphia, Pennsylvania, and Yayla Tribal Rugs, Cambridge, Massachusetts. Finally, I wish to thank my editors, Tina Skinner and Jeffrey Snyder, for their fine work on the manuscript, and my publishers, Peter and Nancy Schiffer, for their early, decisive, and steadfast support for this enterprise.

The foreword was written by Henry Glassie who is the College Professor of Folklore and Co-director of Turkish Studies at Indiana University. His major books include *Turkish Traditional Art Today*, *Art and Life in Bangladesh*, and *The Spirit of Folk Art*.

The Only Good Rug is a Sold Rug
—Anonymous Dealer

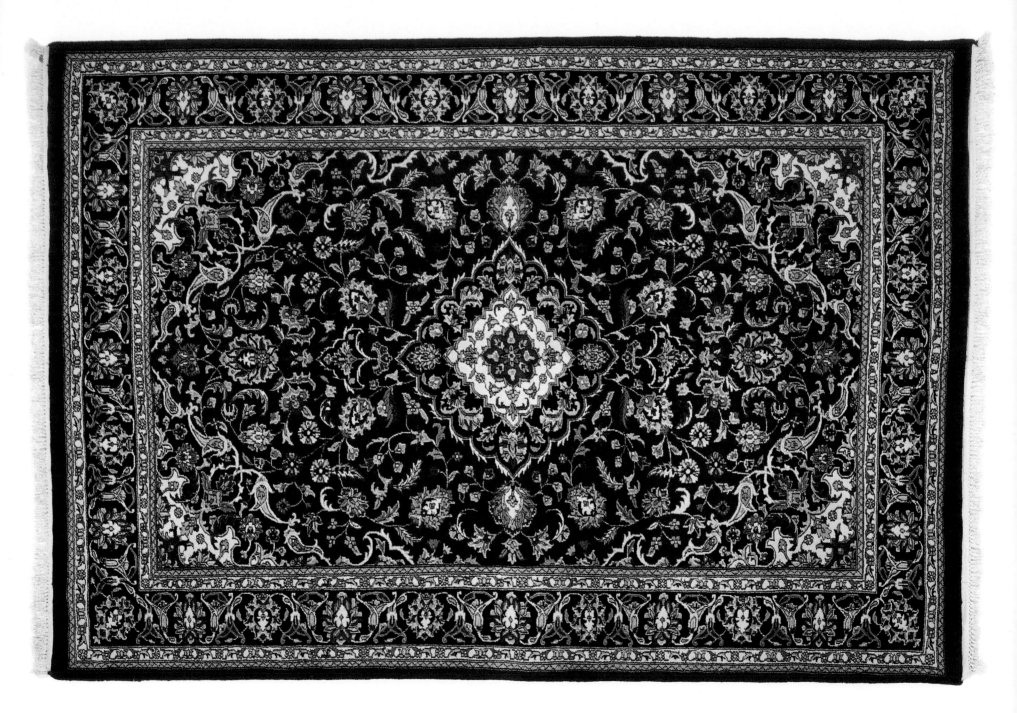

4

Contents

Foreword

Straight talk is this book's virtue. During his years in the trade, Joseph Azizollahoff learned the common concerns and questions of his customers. In this book, speaking without fuss or flourish, he calms the worries, answers the questions, and invites you to participate in the creative system of the oriental carpet.

The carpet's system is anchored in earth. Sheep graze across the land. Through millennia of adaptation, distinct varieties of sheep have evolved that can make it in particular places, usually grassy, rocky, and unfit to plow. The local sheep's wool takes a certain spin, the yarn takes the dye, and it is knotted into designs that are emblems of their place. Working cooperatively at the loom, women weave the carpets that are at once the flower of their environment's potential, symbols of their locality, and embodiments of their own idea of beauty.

The carpet's beauty brings together natural materials, refined to the limit, and the inbuilt dynamic of the human brain, its simultaneous needs for order and play. In its prevailing symmetry, the carpet establishes order. Then in its variety, in its free drawing and whimsical switches of color, the carpet subverts its own order on behalf of delight.

So human a thing, at once disciplined and naughty, teaching its rules and then breaking them — a symphony for the eye that bears meaning as music bears meaning — the carpet is quick to love, impossible to know completely. It is the art of the women of the mountain village, and of the men of the urban workshop, and it has escaped its home in Asia to achieve global appreciation.

In its own place, the carpet is an ecological art, the yield of its environment. Developed in the minds and muscles of its creators, it is a women's art. Expressing afresh the venerable tradition of its locale, the carpet is a folk art. Gathering appreciation through centuries of commerce, finding a place in the black tent of the nomad, in the cozy home of the peasant, in the mosques of the Middle East and the churches of Europe, in the palaces of princes, in the tasteful houses of prosperous people in every land, the carpet is more than a fine art. It is a great art, a marker of humankind, challenged only by Chinese porcelain in the universality of its acceptance.

Beginning on the hazy, gray mountainside, grazed by sheep, ending underfoot in your living room, the carpet generously welcomes diverse interpretation. For the weaver at the loom, it is her work, symbolizing her place, her mother's instruction, her capacity, her aspiration. For the designer in the city atelier, it is a resource for reconfiguration into new elegance. For the dealer, for the old hand in the trade like Joseph Azizollahoff, it is a wonder in its order and variety. It commands his admiration, and it is a commodity that can be sold in confidence, for it will come to rest comfortably in an astonishing range of interiors, it will grow in value, and it will please his customer, building between them a relation of trust, while confirming the possibility of decency in commerce. And for you, the buyer, it can be whatever you wish it to be: sturdy floor covering, or a harmonious complement to a room's decor, or a reminder of cultural diversity and of human unity, or an instance of the human desire for beauty in its boldest, deepest moment. Through care, appreciation, and the stories you tell about your purchases, you become part of the system of creation, a contributor to the master narrative of the oriental carpet.

Joseph Azizollahoff's straight talk clears the way. Shaping his own work out of merchant's lore, answering the customer's common questions, he encourages you to join in the carpet's dance of creation.

— Professor Henry Glassie

Introduction

This book is divided into many discrete sections. The first supply basic, practical information about carpets. The second group of segments describes the imperfections of old rugs and includes drawings to help illustrate defects. The last few divisions are about carpet care.

The chart at the end of the book gives a sense of how a wholesaler categorizes some of the different kinds of old rugs found in the trade. He might classify a piece according to the country, district, town, village, or tribe of origin; therefore, some generic names used by dealers are more specific than others, and one class of carpets listed may be subsumed within a larger grouping catalogued in the table. A little information about each category is included in the chart. Because the data in the table is inferential, exceptions to some of the generalizations may result.

The photographs are an integral part of the book and follow the appropriate sections.

Photographs

The carpets illustrated are samples of the kinds of pieces found in the trade. They were selected for value and attractiveness, as either exemplary or unusual representations of different types of rugs. Most of the old carpets are in very good to excellent condition, but may contain imperfections.

If an old rug is not in excellent condition, the next best thing would be a gently worn carpet with a few low areas where the pile is not quite as long as the nap found in the rest of the piece. This would generally be classified as very good condition for most antique floral, traditional, or formal rugs such as Sarouks, Kermans, and Kashans.

Old geometric, decorative, or informal Heriz, Serape, Mahal, or Oushak carpets are almost never found in perfect condition. Very good condition for these pieces might be characterized by wear in a few small areas with a slight loss of pile on the ends. Worn means no pile covers the foundation, and low means the nap is lower than the rest of the rug. In analyzing condition, more tolerance is given to loosely woven decorative carpets than finely woven traditional pieces, and, consequently, what may be excellent in the former may only be very good or good in the latter. Weavings that are in good condition may contain noticeable, and not insignificant, wear, repair, touchup, discoloration, or pile loss on the ends; however, they are still in fundamentally sound condition. Rugs in fair condition could have several disturbing flaws such as extensive touch-up and heavy wear.

The value of old pieces is difficult to estimate for several reasons. Firstly, some dealers have expenses that are many times higher than others and therefore justifiably charge much higher prices. Secondly, one area of the country or world may have a lower supply and greater demand for certain rugs. Thirdly, some wholesalers are more conservative than others who may pay and charge more for carpets. Finally, relative rarity is unknown, so the same piece might be sold at a higher price by another merchant. Nevertheless, very rough retail prices may be derived from approximate wholesale values. The wholesale value is the maximum an individual dealer will usually pay to purchase a rug from a flea market, auction house, antique store, picker (a dealer who works from his home), private owner, or other merchant. It is also especially important to remember that an old weaving in better condition may be worth much more than a very similar piece in slightly poorer shape if the latter devolves from a good to fair ranking. Differences in condition and quality may not be apparent in the photographs.

It is almost as difficult to estimate the retail value for new carpets as it is for old rugs because overheads vary so greatly. In addition, true innovators invest a lot of time, money, and brain power developing original designs and color combinations, and are justified in charging more for their products. The faithful reproduction of the designs and colors of beautiful antique carpets requires tremendous skill, patience, and artistry. Although producers' markups vary, generally the higher the price the greater the potential collectibility of the piece. New rug values often stem from the subtlety, complexity, and quantity of designs and colors. They are also based upon the quality of the dyes and the length, strength, consistency, and elasticity of all fibers, including cotton.

Size variation causes dramatic differences in the value of old and new carpets.

Most of the new hand- and machine-made rugs, kilims, soumaks, Aubussons, needlepoints, and tapestries illustrated are programmed, or in continuous production, and may be available in other sizes.

In the caption, the letters "c." before the age is an abbreviation for circa, and signifies that the dates are approximate. Sizes and values are also estimates and are marked as such. Sizes are measured in feet and inches so that 5'3" x 6'7" means that the piece measures 5 feet 3 inches by 6 feet 7 inches.

Several photographs of important types of old and new carpets are illustrated to accentuate the significance of certain classes of rugs. The fact that one producer of new carpets has more photographs illustrated than another is not intended as an endorsement of that creator over another.

Chapter 1

Practical Information About Carpets

Rug Weaving

The process of weaving begins with the removal of fleece from the sheep with scissors. The wool is then washed, cleaned, dried, and teased with a comb until it attains a soft, fine appearance similar to cotton candy. At this point, some wool is drawn and spun away from the fine ball of fiber until a thin strand can be attached to a spindle. The spindle is turned by hand, creating yarn and this thread may plied with another to form a stronger fiber. This hand-spun wool is highly desirable and yields a more irregular, roughly textured pile in which individual knots are more visible on the surface of the carpet.

Dying usually involves immersing yarn in a mordant bath such as alum and then steeping it in a boiling dye bath for several hours. When the dyer, a highly skilled craftsman, is finished, the colored wool is dried in the sun.

Tribal looms are simple and portable so they can be readily rolled up and transported from one place to another. Four wooden stakes are often driven into the ground several feet from each other to anchor two horizontal wooden poles that lie flat on the ground opposite one another. Many long warp threads are wrapped around these poles and form part of the foundation of the rug. Several rows of weft shoots are woven over and under alternating warp threads at the end of the loom to provide the foundation for the thousands of tiny knots to follow. When the knotting is completed at the other end, weft threads are again interlaced to bind and finish the carpet.

Village and city or town looms are larger and sturdier than tribal models and are usually upright. These vertical looms have strong side beams to support the opposing horizontal poles. The warp threads are tied around the poles. As the weavers progress, they may hoist themselves higher and higher on a bench until they finish at the top of the rug. Or, the carpet may be rolled up on the floor as more rows of knots are completed. A diagram or cartoon is often placed on the loom for the weavers to follow as they tie the knots.

A knot is made with a small tuft of wool about two inches long that is cut from a skein of yarn, which hangs from the loom. This thread is slipped over, under, and around two warp threads and forms a knot. The knots are looped one by one across the width of the loom. Between each row of knots one or more shoots of weft thread are interlaced across the width to hold the knots in place. The wefts are firmly compressed against the knots with a comb. Slowly, row after row of knots and wefts are completed and the rug is cut off the loom at the ends.

Warp threads may be braided together at the ends of the piece. It is not a flaw if they are bound together in a different manner on each end of the carpet. Then the rug is carefully and evenly sheared by skilled specialist. The finished carpet is finally washed, rinsed, dried, and slightly bleached in the sun to stabilize the dyes before being offered for sale.

Tribal weavings are generally all wool, and village rugs may have wool pile with cotton or wool warps and wefts. Cotton is normally used for the warp and weft in city carpets. Both cotton and wool are highly durable fibers used for the foundation of rugs. Cotton warp fringes are white or grey, and wool fringes may be cream, ivory, brown, or black.

Sizes

Carpets range in size from the pushti of about 2 x 3 feet to very large, room-sized pieces. Standard sizes are 3 x 5, 4 x 6, 5 x 7, 6 x 9, 8 x 10, 9 x 12, 10 x 14, and 12 x 18 feet. They are sold by the square foot, so that a 9 x 12 is 108 square feet. If the piece sells for $30 per square foot, the total cost would be $3,240. It is a good idea to learn the square foot calculation and use it while comparison shopping. Ask the dealer for the price per foot and request the total square footage of the rug. Then simply multiply to get the cost of the carpet. With this figure in hand one can say, "That dealer sells the new 200 line Chinese for $30 a foot. Why is yours $35?" If the dealer says that his piece is a 230 line, which is finer, he should guarantee that in writing.

People generally buy the smallest and least expensive rug that fits the room. Good old 6 x 9 rugs are hard to find because they are in such great demand in retail stores.

In the old carpet trade, interesting, unusual sizes are desirable because they are rare. Coveted sizes include the keilegi, which is about 5 x 10 to 10 x 20 feet; the wide, long runner, which is approximately 5 x 25 feet, and the square, around 8 x 8 feet. The length of the keilegi or gallery rug is usually about two times the width.

In Europe, small pieces up to around 4 x 6 feet are called "rugs" and larger sizes are referred to as "carpets." In the United States both terms are used interchangeably.

Knot Count

High knot count, or knots per square inch, is a positive attribute of formal city carpets. Fineness of weave is less significant in tribal or village weavings where color, character, and vitality are paramount. Herizes, Serapes, Mahals (Sultanabads), Oushaks, and Peking Chinese rugs generally have coarse weaves but may be exceedingly valuable. High knot count usually increases the value of ornate Persian town carpets such as Kashans, Tabrizes, Kermans, and Sarouks as well as their new Indian, Chinese, and Pakistani counterparts. However, many finely woven pieces such as certain new Pakistani Bokkaras and Kashmiri Indians are not valuable because of very thinly spun wool, incomplete knots, or frail foundation. High knot count does not necessarily signify greater durability. Thin, tightly woven rugs are often more delicate than coarse, heavily bodied pieces.

Fineness of weave can be measured by turning over a corner of the carpet and counting the number of knots per square inch on the back. First count the number of knots that run vertically, and then horizontally, with a ruler, and simply multiply. Fine, tightly packed rugs normally have asymmetrical knots with depressed warps. Tufts of wool are wrapped around two warps that are combed so solidly that one warp slips behind the other. When the back of the carpet is viewed, only the wool that enwraps one of the two warps is visible. Many different colored nubs or nodules can be seen on the back of these fine weavings. Each nub represents one knot and colors may change from one nodule to another. Many rugs that are more loosely woven have knots that are partially depressed or not depressed at all. When viewed from the back. each individual knot consists of one and one half or two nubs. In order to measure the knot count, see if the tiniest change of color across a row of knots is composed of more than one nub, and measure accordingly. The back of loosely packed carpets may actually be comprised of more nubs and less knots than one might have initially believed. A weave with up to 50 knots per square inch is coarse, 51 to 150 is medium, and over 150 is fine.

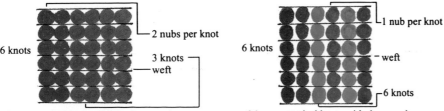

18 symmetrical knots without depressed warps in one square inch of rug viewed from back — two nubs required for each horizontal color change.

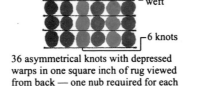

36 asymmetrical knots with depressed warps in one square inch of rug viewed from back — one nub required for each color change.

Age

A good used carpet should look old, particularly if purchased in the West where shoes are commonly worn in the house. Rugs bought in the East do not look as old because shoes are not worn at home. Old carpets have a soft patina with the vitality of harmonized vegetal dyes. Experienced rug lovers generally prefer the holy trinity of colors—natural dyed soft rust, blue, and ivory—commonly found in many of the best antique carpets. Designs should not be blurry, unrefined, or crassly drawn, and patterns and colors should flow into one another harmoniously. Certain old rugs such as Turkish Oushaks, Persian Mahals, and Serapes generally have only a few colors and are quite pale. Although design is quite important, color is probably the most significant element in the appreciation of Oriental carpets. Designs are finite concatenations of color.

Some degree of wear is characteristic of age, but a worn piece is not necessarily old. An antique carpet is defined in the trade as eighty or more years old.

Main field and border designs and colors in quality old rugs are generally balanced. Fairly open center motifs usually coordinate well with moderately sparse border patterns. Busier main-field themes generally complement somewhat more crowded border devices.

Many new carpets are superb copies of classic old pieces. They look just as beautiful when viewed from a distance, but lack power or life when seen up close. Some of the most alluring new weavings have a look and texture that is similar to the most handsome antique carpets even when viewed at a proximate distance. Sometimes new rugs, filled with abrash, or variations in color tone, are misrepresented and sold as antique.

The fashion in the new carpet market today is to chemically wash rugs so that they look antique. Some of these remarkably beautiful, decorative, and popular carpets should be washed less frequently because they may be slightly more delicate than soap or mildly chemical washed rugs. It is best to avoid new weavings where the nap has been excessively buffed or distressed to replicate the wear of antique pieces.

Vegetal, Synthetic, and Chrome Dyes

All the great old rugs from the mid-nineteenth century and earlier were vegetally dyed. Roots, plants, and vegetables formed the basis of colors which mellowed as the carpet developed a patina through wear and exposure to various elements. Natural dying is in fashion today throughout the Near East with the revitalization of traditional methods of making rugs.

The revival of vegetable dying began in Western Turkey in the early 1980s. As antique pieces became more difficult to find, beautiful new rugs were created, mostly in small sizes and in almost every respect similar to antique weavings. A novice looking to develop rug sensibility would be well advised to carefully study contemporary, natural-dyed Turkish village weavings with hand-spun wool.

In general, vegetal dyes are naturally soft even when fully saturated, and they mellow gradually. Natural dyes refract a wide spectrum of light, allowing colors that are almost primary to be pressed together, yielding a harmonious balance. Of all the colors that result from natural dying, green may be the most beautiful. Other desirable hues include yellow, rust, aubergine, camel, and shrimp or coral. A carpet is considered vegetable dyed only if all colors, except indigo or blue, are derived from nature. Synthetic indigo has the same atomic structure as indigo derived from the plant root and is therefore used in many natural-dyed carpets. Some dealers engage in the dubious practice of calling rugs vegetal dyed when they only contain one or two natural dyes.

Early synthetic dyes often ran, corroded wool, changed shades, or faded. Consequently, chemical dyes from the late nineteenth to early twentieth century wrought havoc upon the Oriental carpet trade.

Garish or electric colors are more common in certain synthetically dyed, semi-antique weavings aged forty to sixty years old, and a few contemporary rugs. Certain dark-hued carpets were also woven after 1930 and are not especially valuable even when in excellent condition. Bad colors are often sad, depressing, or triste, and undesirable designs are frequently too busy or dazzling. If one examines, for example, a semi-antique Caucasian Kazak or Shirvan rug and sees bright violet, purple, pink, grape, orange, or yellow colors, the carpet probably has poor synthetic dyes. Muddy browns, murky greys, watery pinks, and an overall dark melancholy appearance, are also signs that bad artificial dyes may have been used. Ironically, some synthetically dyed rugs have desirable, decorative colors such as lilac, taupe, mocha brown, and lavender, and are sought after by interior designers. Semi-antique Turkish Sivas or Kayseri carpets sometimes had unstable dyes. These weavings shouldn't be washed too often so they will fade evenly and not lose too much more color.

Modern chrome dyes were developed around 1950 and utilize potassium dichromate as the mordant which helps the colors adhere to wool. These chemical dyes do not run or damage yarns and are available in numerous different shades. They are more consistent than vegetal dyes and facilitate the programming or replication, of rugs. The main weakness of chrome-dyed wool is that the resulting colors seem to be eternal and do not mellow very much with time. Since chrome dyes have only been in existence for about fifty years, experts do not know how well they will adhere to wool in the next century. Nevertheless, the prognosis is excellent that these dyes will not run, fade, or harm fibers in the future. Most new carpets are chrome dyed.

Appraisals

Appraisals can be done by any reputable dealer in old carpets. One may want an appraisal for insurance purposes, or to gather the knowledge necessary to sell a piece more confidently. The flat fee should be about $150 for the first rug and $30 for each additional piece if one lives fairly near the dealer, slightly more if one is further away. Most dealers with integrity will not try to purchase the carpet unless the client wants to sell, but be leary that some may try very hard to buy it.

The appraisal should consist of a description of the piece including a generic name, origin, size, age, condition, and quality. One may request a written appraisal containing the design description, and retail or replacement valuation, as well as a photograph of the rug.

Before buying a carpet, another dealer may be consulted for appraisal. In order to preclude the possibility of collusion on the part of the dealers involved, do not reveal from whom the rug has been taken on approval. It may be a good idea to not tell the appraising dealer that you are considering buying the piece; rather, you might tell him that it is your own carpet. Otherwise the dealer might denigrate it and try to sell one of his own.

Iran Boycott

Since the hostage crisis in Iran following the fall of the Shah in 1979, the United States government has not permitted any goods from Iran to enter the country. New Iranian or Persian carpets may also not be imported from any other countries. These rugs are brought into the United States illicitly from time to time and are quite cheap. They are often "real" carpets with the soul or vitality lacking in some other contemporary pieces, and may be good investments. However, only those Persian rugs smuggled into the country within the last few years are really good values. Because they were vehicles for removing wealth from Iran, carpets brought by Jews fleeing Khomeini from around 1979 to 1984 are quite expensive. One must weigh the fact that the United States ban on Iranian goods is still in effect when considering whether to buy a Persian rug that has recently appeared in the United States, or a Turkish, Indian, Pakistani, or Chinese carpet.

It is hoped that one day relations with Iran will improve so that beautiful Persian rugs, the staple of imported carpets to the United States for many years, will again be available to the American public.

Buying Abroad

It is generally not advisable to buy rugs on trips to the Near or Far East as few people get good values. Wily salesmen lure visitors into their lairs and use psychology to great effect by reducing prices two to three hundred percent or more before selling the carpet. People typically fare a little better in Europe, but it is usually not a good idea to buy there either.

Purchasing in the United States is preferred because new rugs are imported in large quantities by sea in containers. The improvement in the quality of containers and methods of transport in the last twenty years has made salt water damage unlikely and lowered landed costs considerably. Hooks are not used any more and fork lifts rarely puncture bales of carpets. Home trial and exchangeability make it safer to purchase old rugs locally.

Going Out of Business Sales

In the last fifteen years there has been a rash of going-out-of-business sales in carpets. They have done great damage to the trade because almost all of these sales are merely a way of taking advantage of people who believe they are getting a bargain. Many so called long-established dealers that are closing down are not known to the trade.

The vendor usually takes many rugs from other dealers on consignment, advertises extensively on the radio or in newspapers, and hires a few more workers. Sometimes expensive catalogues are printed with color illustrations and information about carpets. Pieces are marked down seventy percent or more to tempt the public. At the end of the sale, which may go on for several months and include auctions, the retailer opens another store somewhere else under a new name, frequently in the same neighborhood. The more audacious dealers merely change the company's name and keep the same premises. Little is being done by the authorities to curb this form of misrepresentation.

Moving sales are also often bogus because the retailer may decide not to move after all, particularly if he sells a lot of rugs.

In general, going-out-of-business and armory sales have high expenses and offer little benefit to the public. Moving, church, and hotel liquidations, as well as store auctions, are also usually less preferable than buying from reputable wholesalers and retailers of carpets.

Where to Buy

It is safe to buy new carpets from large, established retailers. They allow one to view a variety of pieces, often hanging side by side, in a short period of time. One may also try a number of rugs at home several times, if necessary. This service, and high rent, are very costly for the retailer, and although these expenses are reflected in the price, competition keeps the mark-ups fairly reasonable.

Old pieces should be bought from antique carpet wholesalers and established retailers at or above street level. Some are honest, but others are not, and many simply charge too much. One must slowly and painstakingly shop the market. Dealers who buy for $2,000 to sell for $20,000 feel that they should charge the highest prices they can get and are unethical. Merchants who price their rugs according to their client's wealth, or the cost of the adjacent furniture, are also, unfortunately, found in the trade. They often have a lot of worn, painted pieces and should not be patronized, if possible. The best dealers are very experienced, know value, buy well, and will not sell above a fair price. If the inventory is clean and contains many semi-antique carpets, the dealer is probably a meticulous buyer.

Most old rug wholesalers have good taste, do not make many mistakes in buying, and are delighted to serve individual private buyers who know what they want to acquire. However, many of their carpets are in rough condition. Nowadays, they will normally also allow home trial where condition may be thoroughly evaluated if given a head check or refundable deposit. If the piece is returned in good order, the check is given back to the client. It is not a good idea to go from merchant to merchant trying to determine which antique carpet you like best. One day you may love Bidjars, the next day Kashans, and six months later Herizes, but if you are sure that you especially like Mahals and Oushaks, and have a budget, you may begin to visit the wholesalers.

Reputable dealers will not sell a Kerman whose asking price is $30,000 for $15,000, but will usually agree to a fair price if you are serious about buying. They are highly cognizant of the bottom line, and a reasonable offer is customarily accepted. It is always better, if possible, to pay a little more for an attractive rug in excellent condition than less for a fairly good piece. People sometimes spend too little and are surprised when the carpet doesn't hold its value over time.

Auctions

In recent years auctions have become the paramount source for old carpets. Their influence is so great that they have affected rug valuations within the trade. More people have come to rely upon auctions for buying and selling. Many private buyers have more confidence in buying from auctions than retail stores today even if they have to outbid others for pieces. Although the old carpet market has been quite soft for many years, auctions usually do well, particularly with exceptional weavings.

Auctions may be a little risky unless proper precautions are taken. The desired rug should be viewed front and back, if possible, and condition and valuation should be discussed with the curators. No piece should be purchased unless previewed at the exhibition. Room measurements and color coordination must be exact because carpets may not be returned or exchanged.

Because of the danger of ego involvement in the excitement of the bidding, you should put a cap or maximum on what you are willing to pay, and not go beyond that point. Although it is difficult to follow this stricture, it is the only way to buy effectively at auction. Many people buy at auction on impulse and regret their capriciousness the next day.

It is best to ascertain the type of rug you like, go through the wholesale and retail markets until you have a feel for its value, and then check what the auctions are offering. Auctions should be included among other sources for old carpets.

Estimates of value furnished in the catalogue are usually valid indicators of the fair retail price, but one should not rely exclusively upon the auction house's valuations. Some curators are slightly more conservative than others and, occasionally, estate rugs may have more modest estimates than dealer's carpets.

Most pieces at auction are from dealers, some are from collectors, and only about twenty percent are fresh from estates. Good curators will try to get the lowest reserve or minimum price acceptable to the vendor, but rugs are generally fairly well protected by the seller. The auction's commission is about twenty-five percent, or fifteen percent from the buyer and ten percent or more from the consignor. It is quite possible to get a good value because nice old pieces often aren't bid on by dealers or other private buyers. If the reserve is not too high one may be able to quietly make a very good purchase at auction. It can be more difficult to get a good original estate rug in excellent condition because dealers will usually bid quite strongly for it.

A fine auction gallery may be an excellent place to sell rugs, particularly important collector's or antique tribal and village weavings. Room-sized carpets may also fare well if accepted by a prominent auction house. Smaller galleries and country auctions often accept less valuable pieces if consigned with low reserves. Minor rugs are sometimes sold without reserve protection.

Dr. Thompson's Nomenclature

Although it takes many years to learn to identify rugs according to weave or locale, one can much more readily understand how to categorize them according to the nature of the society in which they were woven and the purpose for which they were made. In his book entitled *Oriental Carpets*, Dr. Jon Thompson classifies rugs as tribal, village or cottage, town or workshop, and court.

Tribal pieces are made by nomads for domestic use and their geometric designs are less impacted by Western commerce and taste. They are there-fore the purest, most primeval weavings, and consequently most coveted by collectors. Antique kilims and old Kurdish, Yoruk, and nomadic Turkoman rugs are examples of the tribal art form.

Village weavings often appear to be similar to tribal carpets, but are made by settled people, and the designs and colors are more influenced by Western trade and aesthetics. When compared with tribal rugs, the patterns may be slightly more derivative or regimented. Many old and new Caucasian and Turkish rugs exemplify this type of cottage industry. Geometric designs are also characteristic of this adaptable kind of craftsmanship.

In both tribal and village carpets, the weaver is essentially the artist or craftsman. However, in town rugs, which are often quite large and fine, made for export, the artist is the designer, and the weaver merely follows a cartoon or diagram. The patterns are generally methodical, rigorously ordered, and uniform. Most new Indian, Pakistani, and Chinese carpets are examples of town weavings. They may have floral or geometric designs.

Court rugs are usually finely woven with highly ornate, curvilinear designs. These opulent rugs were made expressly for early Turkish, Persian, Indian, and Egyptian sultans. They were designed by royal penman and often woven in court sponsored ateliers. Court carpets are rarely found in the trade but can be seen in museums. Extremely fine and elaborate new and old rugs found in the trade, sometimes with silk or metallic thread, are woven in the court style.

Although it is at times difficult to distinguish tribal from village, cottage from workshop, and town from court carpets, it is still a good idea to learn to categorize them according to this methodology.

Design Evolution

Antique rug designs evolved and changed through contact, interaction, and diffusion. This cross-fertilization occurred between neighboring tribes, villages, towns, and courts. Commerce with the West was the joker in the pack that impacted this dialectic significantly for centuries. Scholars are fascinated with these dynamics and try to understand why specific motifs appeared in different, faraway places. Antique Persian Serape designs, for example, were probably derived, in part, from still older Caucasian motifs.

Early floral court designs were sometimes stylized or simplified as they adapted to pre-existing village patterns. The village motifs changed as court designs were assimilated into the peasant culture. These new village patterns intermeshed with other rural designs yielding new forms of ornament. Carpet motifs were borrowed from other media such as textiles, mosque architecture, tilework, pottery, or bookbinding. The aim of much carpet scholarship is to try to determine which medium was most important in the development of specific patterns.

Despite this interaction, rug designs were basically stable, continuous representations of particular locales. They were hallmarks of society and their symmetry and repetitiveness represented the unity and cohesiveness of traditional cultures. Each tribe, village, or town took great pride in the woven insignia they presented to the rest of the world. It is difficult to produce Western-designed carpets to exact specifications in Turkey because weavers do not follow instructions completely and prefer to put their Anatolian imprimatur on the weavings.

Today, some new floral rug designs, created in the West, were derived from antique English textile motifs that were, in turn, influenced by still older Oriental carpet patterns.

New Geometric Rugs

Arguably some of the most extraordinary geometric contemporary weavings are the warm, cheerful, natural-dyed Turkish village rugs and kilims with hand-spun wool. They have become the staple of many of the most prestigious collectors' galleries in the United States and Europe. Because they are often made with beautiful, newly developed vegetal dyes, some of these carpets may be aesthetically superior to many of the best antique rugs. The distance between these weavings and good old pieces is narrow in almost every respect. The carpets with the most potential for becoming collectible antiques normally retail for about $70 per square foot. They may be designed in the West, or indigenous eastern creations that are woven with minimal Western guidance.

The finest producers are frequently innovators who create experimental designs and color combinations that, if successful, are quickly imitated by others. The copies are almost always inferior to the originals. These creative people often have extensive experience in old carpets and restoration.

People should not be afraid of good, strong natural dyes and weavings that are somewhat imposing. Thankfully, Americans, who often cannot get rugs that are pale enough, are beginning to appreciate the beauty of robust, saturated colors.

India has traditionally been the homeland of formal, curvilinear carpets, and is now also a source for some attractive informal and semi-formal geometric pieces with vegetable dyes and hand-spun wool. Look for the best with fair retail prices of approximately $80 a square foot. The colors can be particularly attractive because the natural elements used in dyes from India are different from other countries. Some are heavily, beautifully, and dramatically abrashed, with a variety of tonal variations within the hues.

Excellent, cheerful, thick, and plush rugs are woven by Tibetans and Nepalese in Nepal and generally designed in the West. They are quite popular and frequently have soft, pastel colors and many different patterns, including English Arts and Crafts and purely modern or experimental. Traditional and modern designs are sometimes very successfully combined in the same carpet. Some of the best have hand-spun wool, uncommonly pure designs, and vibrant, deeply saturated chrome dyes. Motifs may also be derived from early Tibetan patterns. Good Tibetan carpets also cost around $70 a square foot at retail and are sound investments.

New Egyptian carpets are among the best natural-dyed geometric weavings on the market today. Their designs are usually derived from antique Persian Mahals, Herizes, or Serapes, Turkish Oushaks, and Indian Agras. They have a dry, granular texture or handle, and the surface of the pile very closely resembles the patina found in old rugs. Some Egyptians have softer and paler colors and retail for about $100 a square foot. Others, with more saturated hues, cost approximately $140 per square foot. Very finely woven carpets as well as unique, special order rugs may have still higher retail prices.

New, soft, natural-dyed Afghan and Pakistan carpets with wool warps and wefts are being produced in traditional Turkoman designs. They are very good values and sometimes come in highly desirable large sizes. They retail for about $40 per square foot and often have the look, feel, and texture of old Turkoman carpets. Other beautiful Afghan weavings have more saturated vegetal dyes and various eastern rug and textile designs.

Certain producers are making the exact same rugs in different countries to precisely equivalent specifications. They will all probably retain comparable value.

New Tibetan carpet. Folk art design woven with minimal Western guidance in Nepal. Vegetal dyes, wool pile, cotton warp and weft, approx. 5' x 6'. *Courtesy of Yayla Tribal Rugs.* Estimated value $1,200.

Left: New Indian carpet. Inspired by old Indian or Persian city carpet. Vegetal dyes, wool pile and weft, cotton warp, approx. 3' 3" x 7' 1". *Courtesy of Samad Brothers, Inc.* Estimated value $2,200.

Right: New Turkish carpet. Folk art design woven with minimal Western guidance. Vegetal dyes, wool pile, cotton warp and weft, approx. 7' 1" x 8' 9". *Courtesy of Woven Legends, Inc.* Estimated value $3,900.

New Indian carpet. Inspired by old Indian or Persian city carpet. Vegetal dyes, wool pile and weft, cotton warp, approx. 3' 5" x 6' 2". *Courtesy of Samad Brothers, Inc.* Estimated value $2,000.

New Turkish carpet. Woven with minimal Western guidance. Vegetal dyes, wool pile, warp, and weft, approx. 4' 2" x 6' 7". *Courtesy of Woven Legends, Inc.* Estimated value $1,000.

New Indian carpet. Folk art design woven with minimal Western guidance. Vegetal dyes, wool pile and weft, cotton warp, approx. 8' 1" x 10' 1". *Courtesy of Samad Brothers, Inc.* Estimated value $7,700.

New Turkish carpet. Woven with minimal Western guidance. Vegetal dyes, wool pile, warp, and weft, approx. 4' 2" x 5' 8". *Courtesy of Woven Legends, Inc.* Estimated value $900.

New Tibetan carpet. Western contemporary design, woven in Nepal. Vegetal dyes, wool pile, cotton warp and weft, approx. 8' x 8'. *Courtesy of Yayla Tribal Rugs.* Estimated value $2,600.

New Turkish carpet. Folk art design woven with minimal Western guidance. Vegetal dyes, wool pile, cotton warp and weft, approx. 6' 6" x 8' 11". *Courtesy of Woven Legends, Inc.* Estimated value $3,600.

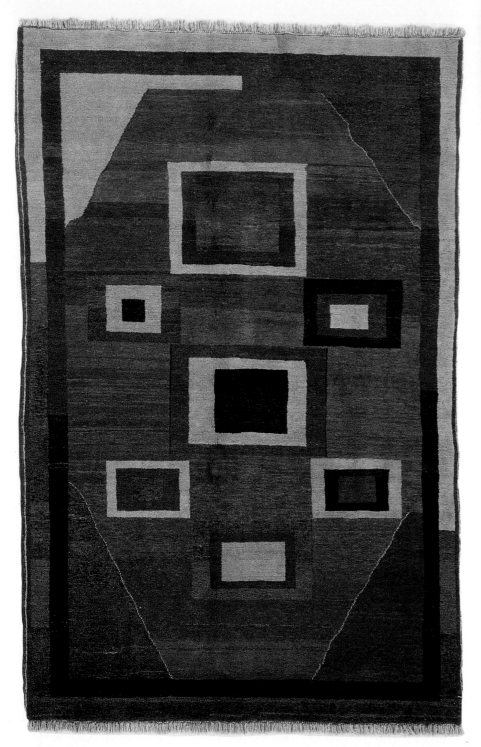

New Turkish carpet. Folk art design woven with minimal Western guidance. Vegetal dyes, wool pile, cotton warp and weft, approx. 6' 2" x 8' 4". *Courtesy of Woven Legends, Inc.* Estimated value $3,200.

New Turkish carpet. Western contemporary design. Vegetal dyes, wool pile, cotton warp and weft, approx. 5' 1" x 8'. *Courtesy of Woven Legends, Inc.* Estimated value $2,500.

New Turkish carpet. Folk art design woven with minimal Western guidance. Vegetal dyes, wool pile, cotton warp and weft, approx. 6' 4" x 7' 11". *Courtesy of Woven Legends, Inc.* Estimated value $3,100.

New Turkish carpet. Folk art design woven with minimal Western guidance. Vegetal dyes, wool pile, cotton warp and weft, approx. 6' x 9' 5". *Courtesy of Woven Legends, Inc.* Estimated value $3,500.

New Turkish carpet. Folk art design woven with minimal Western guidance. Vegetal dyes, wool pile, cotton warp and weft, approx. 8' 1" x 8' 9". *Courtesy of Woven Legends, Inc.* Estimated value $4,400.

New Turkish carpet. Folk art design woven with minimal Western guidance. Vegetal dyes, wool pile, cotton warp and weft, approx. 8' 6" x 10' 4". *Courtesy of Woven Legends, Inc.* Estimated value $5,500.

New Indian carpet. Inspired by old Caucasian Karabagh carpet. Chrome dyes, wool pile, cotton warp and weft, approx. 6' x 9'. *Courtesy of Pande Cameron & Co., Inc.* Estimated value $3,100.

New Turkish carpet. Folk art design woven with minimal Western guidance. Vegetal dyes, wool pile, cotton warp and weft, approx. 8' x 11' 1". *Courtesy of Woven Legends, Inc.* Estimated value $5,500.

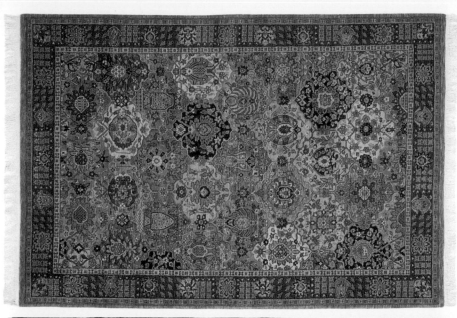

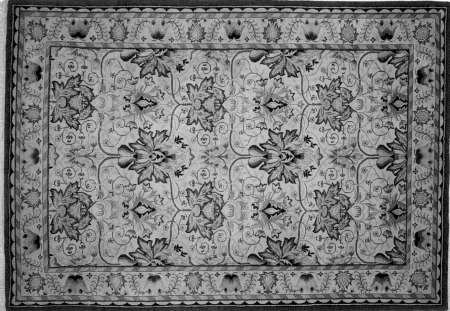

Top left: New Indian carpet. Inspired by Persian Kerman Vase carpet. Chrome dyes, wool pile, cotton warp and weft, approx. 6' x 9'. *Courtesy of Pande Cameron & Co., Inc.* Estimated value $3,100.

Bottom left: New Indian carpet. Inspired by old English Arts and Crafts textile. Chrome dyes, wool pile, cotton warp and weft, approx. 6' x 9'. *Courtesy of Soleimani Rug Co.* Estimated value $2,300.

Right: New Indian carpet. Inspired by old Persian Kerman Vase carpet. Vegetal dyes, wool pile, cotton warp and weft, approx. 6' x 9'. *Courtesy of Harounian Rugs International Co.* Estimated value $2,000.

New Indian carpet. Inspired by old Persian Herat carpet. Vegetal dyes, wool pile, cotton warp and weft, approx. 6' 10" x 10' 3". *Courtesy of Woven Legends, Inc./Michaelian & Kohlberg, Inc.* Estimated value $4,400.

New Turkish carpet. Inspired by old Persian Serape carpet. Vegetal dyes, wool pile, cotton warp and weft, approx. 6' 8" x 9' 10". *Courtesy of Woven Legends, Inc.* Estimated value $4,100.

New Tibetan carpet. Inspired by old Turkish Oushak carpet, woven in Nepal. Chrome and vegetal dyes, wool pile, cotton warp and weft, approx. 8' x 10'. *Courtesy of Michaelian & Kohlberg, Inc.* Estimated value $5,600.

New Indian carpet. Inspired by old Indian or Persian city carpet. Vegetal dyes, wool pile and weft, cotton warp, approx. 6' 1" x 12' 2". *Courtesy of Samad Brothers, Inc.* Estimated value $7,000.

New Tibetan carpet. Inspired by old Spanish carpet, woven in Nepal. Chrome and vegetal dyes, wool pile, cotton warp and weft, approx. 8' x 10'. *Courtesy of Michaelian & Kohlberg, Inc.* Estimated value $5,600.

New Afghanistan carpet. Inspired by old Persian Serape carpet. Vegetal dyes, wool pile, cotton warp and weft, approx. 10' x 10'. *Courtesy of Yayla Tribal Rugs.* Estimated value $6,000.

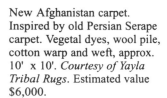

New Indian carpet. Inspired by old Persian Bidjar carpet. Vegetal dyes, wool pile, cotton warp and weft, approx. 9' x 11'. *Courtesy of Woven Legends, Inc.* Estimated value $6,200.

New Indian carpet. Inspired by old Persian Serape carpet. Chrome dyes, wool pile, cotton warp and weft, approx. 8' x 10'. *Courtesy of Lotfy & Sons, Inc.* Estimated value $5,000.

New Egyptian carpet.
Inspired by old Indian Agra
carpet. Vegetal dyes, wool
pile, cotton warp and weft,
approx. 10' x 10'. *Courtesy
of Iraj Fine Oriental Rugs,
Inc*. Estimated value
$10,000.

New Indian carpet. Inspired by old Persian Heriz carpet. Chrome dyes, wool pile, cotton warp and weft, approx. 9' x 12'. *Courtesy of Fazeli/Trans Orient, Inc.* Estimated value $4,700.

New Turkish carpet. Inspired by old Turkish kilim. Vegetal dyes, wool pile, cotton warp and weft, approx. 7' 8" x 9' 11". *Courtesy of Woven Legends, Inc.* Estimated value $4,800.

New Turkish carpet. Inspired by old Persian Heriz carpet. Vegetal dyes, wool pile, cotton warp and weft, approx. 9' 6" x 12' 3". *Courtesy of Woven Legends, Inc.* Estimated value $7,300.

New Turkish carpet. Inspired by old Persian Bakshaiash carpet. Cypress and weeping willow tree designs. Vegetal dyes, wool pile, cotton warp and weft, approx. 9' 5" x 12' 9". *Courtesy of Woven Legends, Inc.* Estimated value $7,500.

New Turkish carpet. Inspired by old Persian Heriz carpet. Vegetal dyes, wool pile, cotton warp and weft, approx. 9' 11" x 11'. *Courtesy of Woven Legends, Inc.* Estimated value $6,800.

Right: New Indian carpet. Inspired by old Persian Serape carpet. Chrome dyes, wool pile, cotton warp and weft, approx. 9' x 12'. *Courtesy of Fazeli/Trans Orient, Inc.* Estimated value $4,700.

New Indian carpet. Inspired by old Persian Herat carpet. Vegetal dyes, wool pile, cotton warp and weft, approx. 9' x 12'. *Courtesy of Woven Legends, Inc./Michaelian & Kohlberg, Inc.* Estimated value $6,800.

New Turkish carpet. Inspired by old Persian Qashqai carpet. Vegetal dyes, wool pile, cotton warp and weft, approx. 9' 7" x 15' 8". *Courtesy of Woven Legends, Inc./Michaelian & Kohlberg, Inc.* Estimated value $9,400.

New Indian carpet. Inspired by old Persian Kerman Vase carpet. Vegetal dyes, wool pile, cotton warp and weft, approx. 6' x 18'. *Courtesy of Woven Legends, Inc./Michaelian & Kohlberg, Inc.* Estimated value $6,800.

New Turkish carpet. Inspired by old Persian Serape carpet. Vegetal dyes, wool pile, cotton warp and weft, approx. 9' 8" x 13' 7". *Courtesy of Woven Legends, Inc.* Estimated value $8,200.

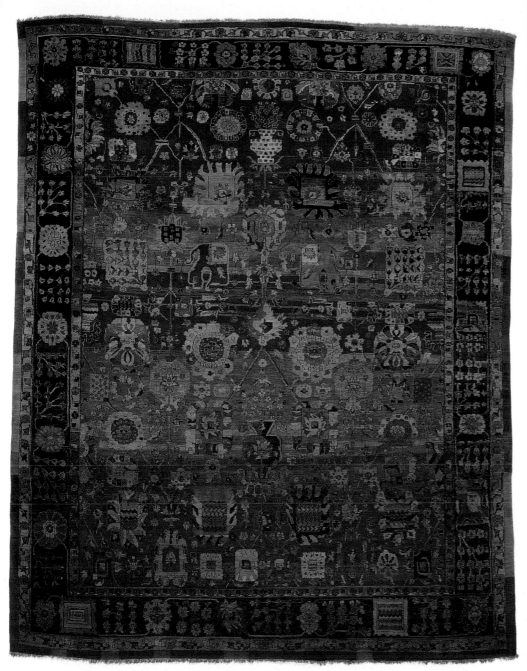

New Indian carpet. Inspired by old Persian Kerman Vase carpet. Vegetal dyes, wool pile and weft, cotton warp, approx. 9' 8" x 13' 9". *Courtesy of Samad Brothers, Inc.* Estimated value $12,500.

New Turkish carpet. Inspired by old Persian Sultanabad carpet. Vegetal dyes, wool pile, cotton warp and weft, approx. 9' 6" x 13' 10". *Courtesy of Woven Legends, Inc./ Michaelian & Kohlberg, Inc.* Estimated value $8,200.

New Turkish carpet. Inspired by old Persian Bakshaiash carpet. Vegetal dyes, wool pile, cotton warp and weft, approx. 9' 9" x 13'. *Courtesy of Woven Legends, Inc.* Estimated value $8,000.

New Indian carpet. Inspired by old Indian Agra carpet. Chrome dyes, wool pile, cotton warp and weft, approx. 10' x 14'. *Courtesy of Global Rug Corp./Woven Arts, Inc.* Estimated value $11,000.

New Turkish carpet. Inspired by old Persian Sultanabad carpet. Vegetal dyes, wool pile, cotton warp and weft, approx. 11' 3" x 14' 7". *Courtesy of Woven Legends, Inc./Michaelian & Kohlberg, Inc.* Estimated value $10,000.

New Turkish carpet. Inspired by old Irish Arts and Crafts carpet. Vegetal dyes, wool pile, cotton warp and weft, approx. 12' 6" x 13' 3". *Courtesy of Woven Legends, Inc./Michaelian & Kohlberg, Inc.* Estimated value $10,500.

New Chinese carpet. Inspired by old Persian Mohtesham Kashan carpet. Vegetal dyes, wool pile, cotton warp and weft, approx. 11' 10" x 14' 10". *Courtesy of Woven Legends, Inc./ Michaelian & Kohlberg, Inc.* Estimated value $13,000.

New Turkish carpet. Inspired by old Persian Sultanabad carpet. Vegetal dyes, wool pile, cotton warp and weft, approx. 10' 8" x 15' 10". *Courtesy of Woven Legends, Inc./ Michaelian & Kohlberg, Inc.* Estimated value $10,500.

New Egyptian carpet. Inspired by old Persian Sultanabad carpet. Vegetal dyes, wool pile, cotton warp and weft, approx. 12' 5" x 16' 10". *Courtesy of Christie's, Inc.* Estimated value $21,000.

New Egyptian carpet. Inspired by old Persian Sultanabad carpet. Vegetal dyes, wool pile, cotton warp and weft, approx. 12' x 16'. *Courtesy of Iraj Fine Oriental Rugs, Inc.* Estimated value $19,000.

New Tibetan carpet. Inspired by modern art designs, woven in Nepal. Chrome and vegetal dyes, wool pile, cotton warp and weft, approx. 4' x 6'. *Courtesy of Michaelian & Kohlberg, Inc.* Estimated value $1,900.

New Tibetan carpet. Western contemporary design, woven in Nepal. Chrome dyes, wool pile, cotton warp and weft, approx. 4' x 6'. *Courtesy of Odegard, Inc.* Estimated value $1,200.

New Tibetan carpet. Inspired by old Tibetan carpet, woven in Nepal. Chrome dyes, wool pile, cotton warp and weft, approx. 3' 6" x 5' 6". *Courtesy of Odegard, Inc.* Estimated value $1,900.

Above: New Tibetan carpet. Inspired by old Tibetan carpet, woven in Nepal. Chrome dyes, wool pile, cotton warp and weft, approx. 2' 8" x 6' 5". *Courtesy of Odegard, Inc.* Estimated value $1,700.

Opposite page:
Left: New Turkish carpet. Inspired by old Persian Bidjar carpet. Vegetal dyes, wool pile, cotton warp and weft, approx. 12' 1" x 19' 1". *Courtesy of Woven Legends, Inc.* Estimated value $14,500.
Right: New Indian carpet. Inspired by old Turkish Oushak carpet. Chrome dyes, wool pile, cotton warp and weft, approx. 12' x 18'. *Courtesy of Global Rug Corp./Woven Arts, Inc.* Estimated value $11,000.

Top right: New Tibetan carpet. Western contemporary design, woven in Nepal. Chrome dyes, wool pile, cotton warp and weft, approx. 4' x 6'. *Courtesy of Odegard, Inc.* Estimated value $1,200.

Bottom right: New Tibetan carpet. Western contemporary design, woven in Nepal. Chrome dyes, wool pile, cotton warp and weft, approx. 6' x 9'. *Courtesy of Odegard, Inc.* Estimated value $3,200.

Center: New Tibetan carpet. Western contemporary design, woven in Nepal. Chrome dyes, wool pile, cotton warp and weft, approx. 2' 8" x 10'. *Courtesy of Odegard, Inc.* Estimated value $1,300.

Opposite page:
Left: New Tibetan carpet. Inspired by old Tibetan doorway carpet, woven in Nepal. Chrome dyes, wool pile, cotton warp and weft, approx. 3' x 8'. *Courtesy of Odegard, Inc.* Estimated value $2,400.

Center: Two new Tibetan carpets. Inspired by old Tibetan doorway carpets, woven in Nepal. Chrome dyes, wool pile, cotton warp and weft, approx. 2'8" x 9' each. *Courtesy of Odegard, Inc.* Estimated value $2,400 each.

Right: New Tibetan carpet. Inspired by Chinese/Mongolian designs, woven in Nepal. Chrome dyes, wool pile, cotton warp and weft, approx. 2' 6" x 8'. *Courtesy of Odegard, Inc.* Estimated value $2,000.

39

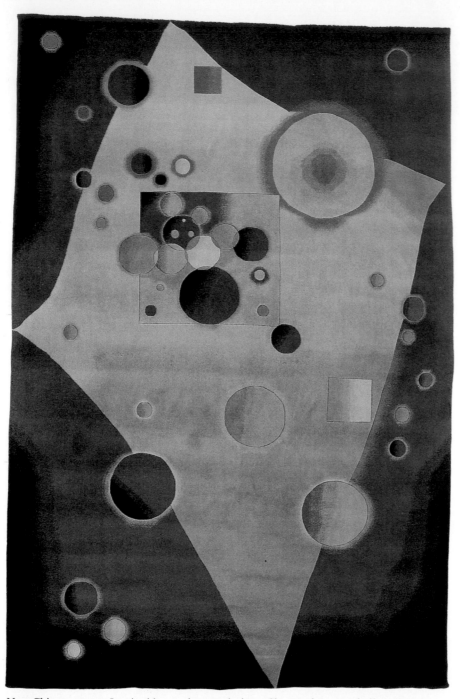

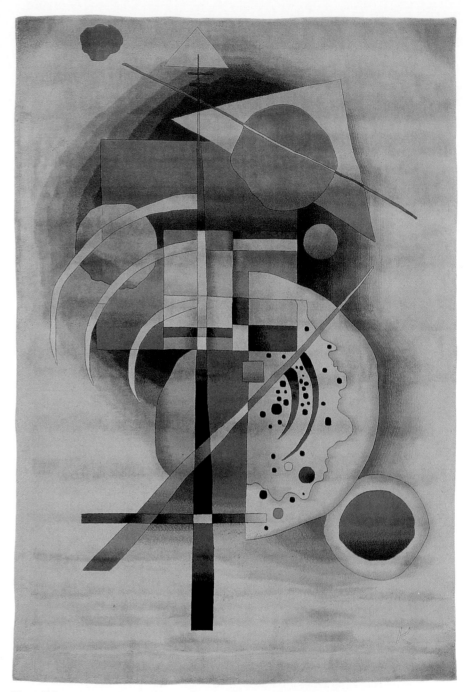

New Chinese carpet. Inspired by modern art designs. Chrome dyes, wool pile, cotton warp and weft, approx. 5' 9" x 8' 9". *Courtesy of Nourison Rug Corp.* Estimated value $2,100.

New Chinese carpet. Inspired by modern art designs. Chrome dyes, wool pile, cotton warp and weft, approx. 5' 9" x 8' 9". *Courtesy of Nourison Rug Corp.* Estimated value $2,100.

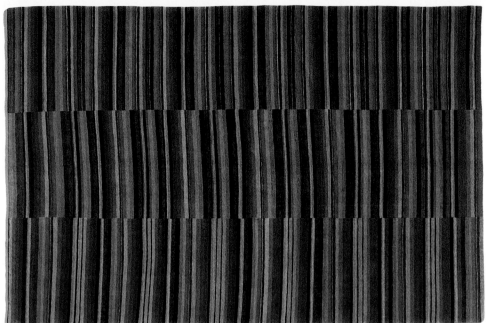

New Tibetan carpet. Inspired by old Tibetan textile, woven in Nepal. Chrome dyes, wool pile, cotton warp and weft, approx. 6' x 9'. *Courtesy of Odegard, Inc.* Estimated value $5,400.

New Chinese carpet. Inspired by Art Deco designs. Chrome dyes, wool pile, cotton warp and weft, approx. 7' 9" x 9' 9". *Courtesy of Nourison Rug Corp.* Estimated value $2,500.

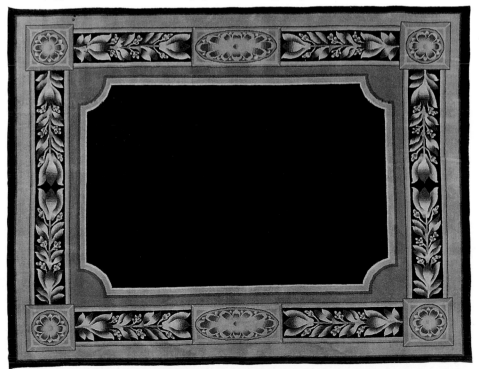

New Tibetan carpet. Western contemporary shell design, woven in Nepal. Chrome dyes, wool pile, cotton warp and weft, approx. 6' x 9'. *Courtesy of Odegard, Inc.* Estimated value $5,400.

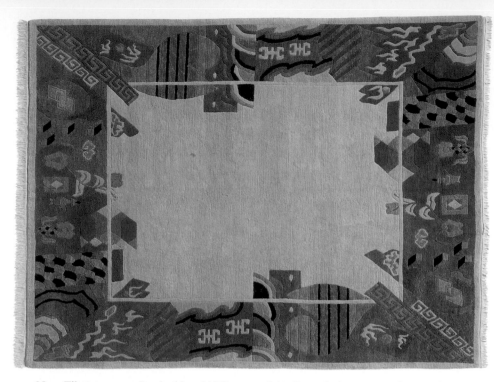

New Tibetan carpet. Inspired by old Tibetan and Art Deco designs, woven in Nepal. Chrome dyes, wool pile, cotton warp and weft, approx. 8' x 10'. *Courtesy of Odegard, Inc.* Estimated value $4,800.

New Tibetan carpet. Inspired by old Japanese textile, woven in Nepal. Vegetal dyes, wool pile, cotton warp and weft, approx. 8' x 10'. *Courtesy of Odegard, Inc.* Estimated value $5,600.

New Tibetan carpet. Western contemporary design, woven in Nepal. Chrome and vegetal dyes, wool pile, cotton warp and weft, approx. 8' x 10'. *Courtesy of Michaelian & Kohlberg, Inc.* Estimated value $5,600.

Above: New Tibetan carpet. Western contemporary design, woven in Nepal. Chrome dyes, wool pile, cotton warp and weft, approx. 8' x 10'. *Courtesy of Odegard, Inc.* Estimated value $4,800.

New Tibetan carpet. Western contemporary design, woven in Nepal. Chrome dyes, wool pile, cotton warp and weft, approx. 9' x 12'. *Courtesy of Odegard, Inc.* Estimated value $6,500.

New Tibetan carpet. Western contemporary design, woven in Nepal. Chrome and vegetal dyes, wool pile, cotton warp and weft, approx. 9' x 12'. *Courtesy of Odegard, Inc.* Estimated value $11,000.

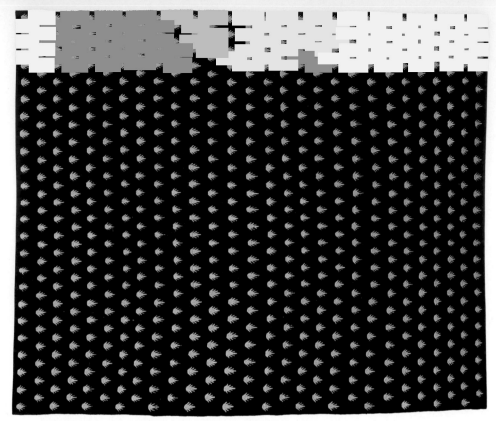

New Tibetan carpet. Inspired by old Chinese/Tibetan flame design, woven in Nepal. Chrome dyes, wool pile, cotton warp and weft, approx. 9' x 12'. *Courtesy of Odegard, Inc.* Estimated value $11,000.

New Floral Rugs

New carpets are a safer purchase than old because, in general, there are no condition problems. This epoch may be a golden age of contemporary formal, floral, or curvilinear rugs from India, Pakistan, and China as business has burgeoned tenfold in the last thirty years. The color combinations are normally excellent because designers with fine arts degrees are often involved in production and the quality control is usually superb. Many highly experienced producers and importers of these carpets in New York City today were formerly merchants in the Tehran bazaar in Iran. Some of the more imaginative dealers are also innovators who create new patterns and hues within a traditional context.

Because of the great efforts made by Western producers to achieve perfect harmony between design and color, these copies of classical Iranian carpets deserve a lot of respect. Only negligible variations are acceptable in most formal rugs from India, Pakistan, and China such as very subtle abrash or change within certain colors. Curves, bumps, and weave irregularities that used to be characteristic of the carpets from Iran, Turkey, and Afghanistan are unforgivable in these more mechanized productions. Quality control is improving today even in the weavings from Iran, Turkey, and Afghanistan. Sturdier looms have greatly reduced the number of imperfections that were characteristic years ago.

Two disadvantages of rugs from India, Pakistan, and China are that the designs are sometimes too mechanical and the colors, occasionally, somewhat dull. In seeking contemporary weavings from these countries, try to find examples that are very fine and beautiful to offset the drawbacks of mass production. Some of the best new carpets from Pakistan have traditional Persian designs and thick, hard backs. These finely woven pieces retail for about $80 a square foot and should hold value if well preserved. The best Indian carpets are usually thick, heavy, and strong, and the most desirable Chinese rugs are generally thin, fine, and delicate.

Superb copies of antique Indian Agra carpets in stylized-floral designs are being produced in various workshops in India today. The finest retail for around $80 to $100 a square foot. Exact reproductions of old Indian Amritsars are also available for approximately $80 a square foot.

Admirable work has been done to develop replicas of antique French Savonnerie rugs in Romania and China. The Romanian carpets have a fairly dry handle or texture and are made with strong Balkan wool. These weavings are superior to many semi-antique Savonneries from Europe. The yarns frequently have many shades of color, and rugs vary, according to quality, from about $60 to $80 a square foot at retail. Some new Savonneries from China have a thick, smoothly textured, wool from New Zealand. The designs are especially intricate and often contain numerous shades of closely related colors. These formal replicas of the most coveted antique European rugs retail for approximately $150 a square foot.

The computer is now being utilized in the development of innovative carpet patterns. It has opened the possibility for producers to create extremely complex designs in their offices. Computer assisted ornamentation tends to be highly symmetrical and angular. Some weavings have a digital, grid-like sensibility, and very subtle gradations of color. The patterns of the most successful rugs are not too busy and the colors flow harmoniously into one another. The exceptional detail compensates for the severity of some of the designs.

Above: New Indian carpet. Inspired by old Indian Agra carpet. Prayer design. Chrome dyes, wool pile, cotton warp and weft, approx. 7' x 8'. *Courtesy of Samad Brothers, Inc.* Estimated value $4,500.

Below: New Indian carpet. Inspired by old Indian Agra carpet. Vegetal dyes, wool pile, cotton warp and weft, approx. 6' x 9'. *Courtesy of Harounian Rugs International Co.* Estimated value $2,000.

New Indian carpet. Inspired by old Persian Shah Abbas carpet. Chrome dyes, wool pile, cotton warp and weft, approx. 6' x 9'. *Courtesy of Soleimani Rug Co.* Estimated value $2,500.

New Indian carpet. Inspired by old Persian Khorassan carpet in the Winterthur Museum collection. Chrome dyes, wool pile, cotton warp and weft, approx. 6' x 9'. *Courtesy of Pande Cameron & Co., Inc.* Estimated value $3,000.

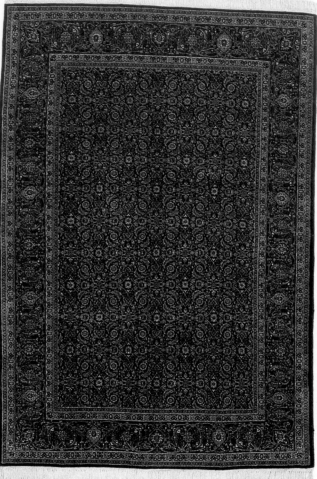

New Indian carpet. Inspired by old Persian Tabriz carpet. Herati design. Chrome dyes, wool pile, cotton warp and weft, approx. 6' x 9'. *Courtesy of Pande Cameron & Co., Inc.* Estimated value $3,500.

New Indian carpet. Inspired by old Persian Kerman carpet. Chrome dyes, wool pile, cotton warp and weft, approx. 6' x 9'. *Courtesy of Pande Cameron & Co., Inc.* Estimated value $3,500.

Right: New Indian carpet. Inspired by old Persian Kashan carpet. Chrome dyes, wool pile, cotton warp and weft, approx. 6' x 9'. *Courtesy of Aminco, Inc.* Estimated value $2,200.

Above: New Indian carpet. Inspired by old Persian Qum carpet. Chrome dyes, wool pile, cotton warp and weft, approx. 6' x 9' *Courtesy of Pande Cameron & Co., Inc.* Estimated value $3,100.

Below: New Indian carpet. Inspired by old Persian Kashan carpet. Chrome dyes, wool pile, cotton warp and weft, approx. 6' x 9'. *Courtesy of Harounian Rugs International Co.* Estimated value $2,000.

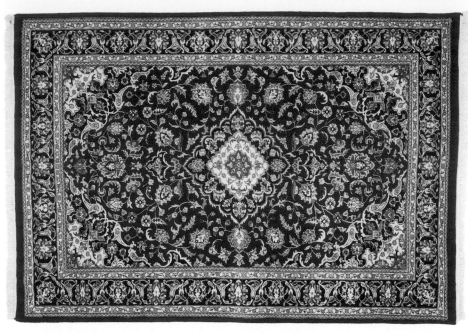

New Indian carpet. Inspired by old Persian Kashan carpet. Chrome dyes, wool pile, cotton warp and weft, approx. 6' x 9'. *Courtesy of Harounian Rugs International Co.* Estimated value $2,000.

Above: New Indian carpet. Inspired by old French Aubusson flatweave. Chrome dyes, wool pile, cotton warp and weft, approx. 6' x 9'. *Courtesy of Pande Cameron & Co., Inc.* Estimated value $2,700.

Right: New Indian carpet. Inspired by old Persian Kashan carpet. Chrome dyes, wool pile, cotton warp and weft, approx. 6' x 9'. *Courtesy of Pande Cameron & Co., Inc.* Estimated value $4,500.

New Indian carpet. Inspired by old French Aubusson flatweave. Chrome dyes, wool pile, cotton warp and weft, approx. 6' x 9'. *Courtesy of Pande Cameron & Co., Inc.* Estimated value $2,700.

New Pakistan carpet. Inspired by old French Aubusson flatweave. Chrome dyes, wool pile, cotton warp and weft, approx. 8' x 10'. *Courtesy of Lotfy & Sons, Inc.* Estimated value $5,500.

New Pakistan carpet. Inspired by old French Aubusson flatweave. Chrome dyes, wool pile, cotton warp and weft, approx. 8' x 10'. *Courtesy of Noonoo Rug Co., Inc.* Estimated value $8,000.

49

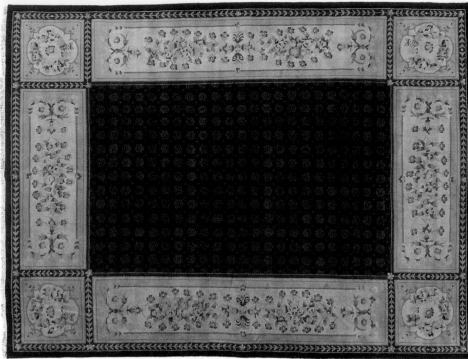

Right: New Chinese carpet. Inspired by old Nichols Chinese carpet. Chrome dyes, wool pile, cotton warp and weft, approx. 7' 9" x 9' 9". *Courtesy of Nourison Rug Corp.* Estimated value $2,500.

Below: New Indian carpet. Inspired by old European floral designs. Chrome dyes, wool pile, cotton warp and weft, approx. 8' x 10'. *Courtesy of Soleimani Rug Co.* Estimated value $2,500.

Above: New Chinese carpet. Inspired by old French Aubusson flatweave. Chrome dyes, wool pile, cotton warp and weft, approx. 8' 6" x 11' 6". *Courtesy of Nourison Rug Corp.* Estimated value $3,100.

Left: New Chinese carpet. Inspired by old Nichols Chinese carpet. Chrome dyes, wool pile, cotton warp and weft, approx. 7' 9" x 9' 9". *Courtesy of Nourison Rug Corp.* Estimated value $2,500.

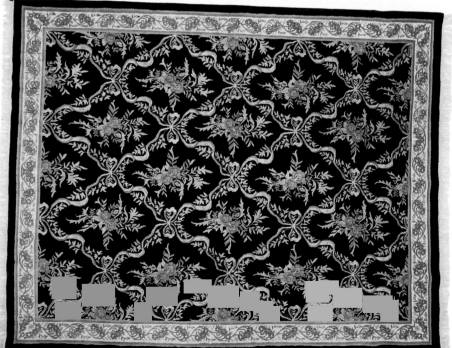

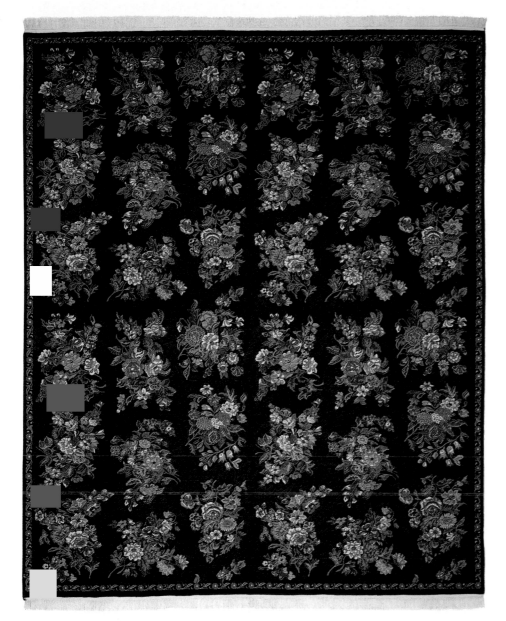

New Pakistan carpet. Inspired by old European floral designs. Chrome dyes, wool pile, cotton warp and weft, approx. 8' x 10'. *Courtesy of Noonoo Rug Co., Inc.* Estimated value $8,000.

New Pakistan carpet. Inspired by old European floral designs. Chrome dyes, wool pile, cotton warp and weft, approx. 8' x 10'. *Courtesy of Noonoo Rug Co., Inc.* Estimated value $8,000.

New Indian carpet. Inspired by old English textile. Chrome dyes, wool pile, cotton warp and weft, approx. 8' x 10'. *Courtesy of Samad Brothers, Inc.* Estimated value $6,400.

New Indian carpet. Inspired by old English textile. Chrome dyes, wool pile, cotton warp and weft, approx. 8' x 10'. *Courtesy of Samad Brothers, Inc.* Estimated value $6,400.

New Indian carpet. Inspired by old English textile. Chrome dyes, wool pile, cotton warp and weft, approx. 8' x 10'. *Courtesy of Samad Brothers, Inc.* Estimated value $6,400.

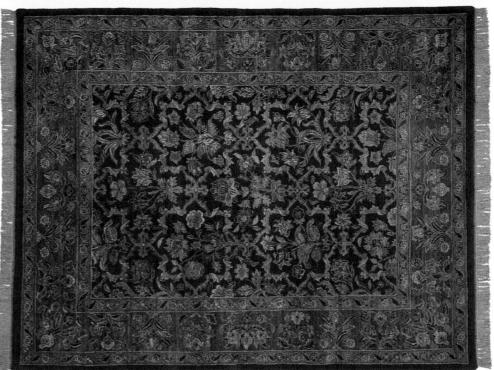

New Indian carpet. Inspired by old Indian Moghul court carpet. Chrome dyes, wool pile, cotton warp and weft, approx. 8' x 10'. *Courtesy of Samad Brothers, Inc.* Estimated value $6,400.

New Indian carpet. Inspired by old English textile. Chrome dyes, wool pile, cotton warp and weft, approx. 8' x 10'. *Courtesy of Samad Brothers, Inc.* Estimated value $6,400.

New Indian carpet. Inspired by old Persian Herat carpet. Chrome dyes, wool pile, cotton warp and weft, approx. 8' x 10'. *Courtesy of Global Rug Corp./Woven Arts, Inc.* Estimated value $4,200.

Above: New Indian carpet. Inspired by old Persian Bidjar carpet. Chrome dyes, wool pile, cotton warp and weft, approx. 8' x 10'. *Courtesy of Soleimani Rug Co.* Estimated value $3,500.

Top right: New Indian carpet. Inspired by old Persian Isfahan carpet. Chrome dyes, wool pile, cotton warp and weft, approx. 8' x 10'. *Courtesy of Aminco, Inc.* Estimated value $3,200.

Bottom right: New Indian carpet. Inspired by old Persian Veramin carpet. Chrome dyes, wool pile, cotton warp and weft, approx. 8' x 10'. *Courtesy of Soleimani Rug Co.* Estimated value $3,200.

New Indian carpet. Inspired by old Persian Qum silk carpet. Chrome dyes, wool pile, cotton warp and weft, approx. 8' x 10'. *Courtesy of Aminco, Inc.* Estimated value $3,600.

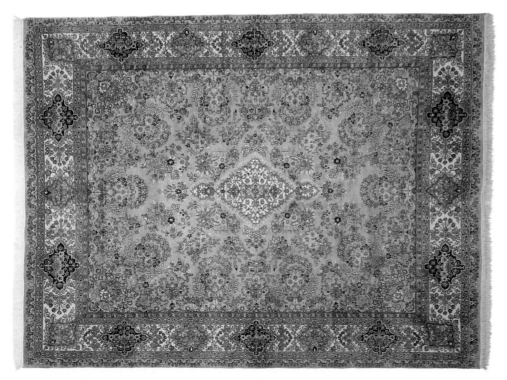

New Pakistan carpet. Inspired by old Persian Kashan carpet. Chrome dyes, wool pile, cotton warp and weft, approx. 8' x 10'. *Courtesy of Noonoo Rug Co., Inc.* Estimated value $8,000.

New Indian carpet. Inspired by old Persian Kerman carpet. Chrome dyes, wool pile, cotton warp and weft, approx. 8' x 10'. *Courtesy of Aminco, Inc.* Estimated value $3,200.

New Pakistan carpet. Inspired by old Persian Lavar Kerman carpet. Chrome dyes, wool pile, cotton warp and weft, approx. 8' x 10'. *Courtesy of Noonoo Rug Co., Inc.* Estimated value $8,000.

New Indian carpet. Inspired by old Persian Lavar Kerman carpet. Chrome dyes, wool pile, cotton warp and weft, approx. 8' x 10'. *Courtesy of Soleimani Rug Co.* Estimated value $5,000.

Above: New Indian carpet. Inspired by old Persian Kerman carpet. Chrome dyes, wool pile, cotton warp and weft, approx. 8' 6" x 11' 6". *Courtesy of Nourison Rug Corp.* Estimated value $2,800.
Below: New Indian carpet. Inspired by old Persian Kerman carpet. Chrome dyes, wool pile, cotton warp and weft, approx. 9' x 12'. *Courtesy of Harounian Rugs International Co.* Estimated value $4,000.

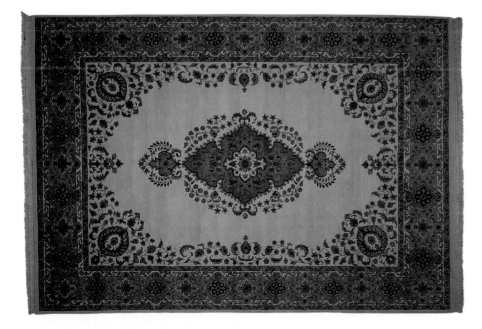

New Indian carpet. Inspired by old Persian Kerman carpet. Chrome dyes, wool pile, cotton warp and weft, approx. 9' x 12'. *Courtesy of Pande Cameron & Co., Inc.* Estimated value $9,000.

New Indian carpet. Inspired by old Persian Lillihan carpet. Chrome dyes, wool pile, cotton warp and weft, approx. 9' x 12'. *Courtesy of Fazeli/Trans Orient, Inc.* Estimated value $4,000.

Above: New Indian carpet. Inspired by old Persian Tabriz carpet. Chrome dyes, wool pile, cotton warp and weft, approx. 9' x 12'. *Courtesy of Fazeli/Trans Orient, Inc.* Estimated value $6,000.
Right: New Indian carpet. Inspired by old Persian Sarouk carpet. Chrome dyes, wool pile, cotton warp and weft, approx. 9' x 12'. *Courtesy of Harounian Rugs International Co.* Estimated value $4,000.

Above: New Indian carpet. Inspired by old Persian Sarouk carpet. Chrome dyes, wool pile, cotton warp and weft, approx. 9' x 12'. *Courtesy of Fazeli/Trans Orient, Inc.* Estimated value $6,000.

Below: New Indian carpet. Inspired by old Persian Ferahan Sarouk carpet. Chrome dyes, wool pile, cotton warp and weft, approx. 9' x 12'. *Courtesy of Fazeli/Trans Orient, Inc.* Estimated value $6,000.

New Indian carpet. Inspired by old Persian Ferahan Sarouk carpet. Chrome dyes, wool pile, cotton warp and weft, approx. 10' x 14'. *Courtesy of Global Rug Corp./Woven Arts, Inc.* Estimated value $10,000.

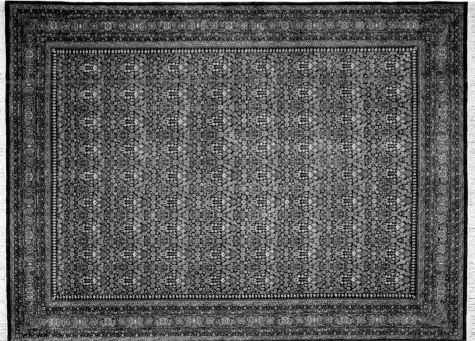

New Chinese carpet. Inspired by old Persian Mohtesham Kashan carpet. Vegetal dyes, wool pile, cotton warp and weft, approx. 10' 9" x 13' 4". *Courtesy of Woven Legends, Inc./Michaelian & Kohlberg, Inc.* Estimated value $10,500.

New Indian carpet. Inspired by old French Art Nouveau carpet. Vegetal dyes, wool pile, cotton warp and weft, approx. 9' 2" x 13' 3". *Courtesy of Woven Legends, Inc./Michaelian & Kohlberg, Inc.* Estimated value $7,600.

New Indian carpet. Inspired by old Indian Moghul court carpet. Chrome dyes, wool pile, cotton warp and weft, approx. 10' x 14'. *Courtesy of Global Rug Corp./Woven Arts, Inc.* Estimated value $11,000.

New Indian carpet. Inspired by old Indian Amritsar carpet. Chrome dyes, wool pile, cotton warp and weft, approx. 10' x 14'. *Courtesy of Global Rug Corp./Woven Arts, Inc.* Estimated value $11,000.

61

New Indian carpet. Inspired by old Indian Moghul court carpet. Chrome dyes, wool pile, cotton warp and weft, approx. 10' x 12'. *Courtesy of Global Rug Corp./Woven Arts, Inc.* Estimated value $9,500.

New Indian carpet. Inspired by old Indian Moghul court carpet. Chrome dyes, wool pile, cotton warp and weft, approx. 10' x 14'. *Courtesy of Global Rug Corp./Woven Arts, Inc.* Estimated value $12,000.

New Indian carpet. Inspired by old Persian Ferahan Sarouk carpet. Chrome dyes, wool pile, cotton warp and weft, approx. 12' x 15'. *Courtesy of Global Rug Corp./Woven Arts, Inc.* Estimated value $13,000.

New Indian carpet. Inspired by old Persian Kashan carpet. Chrome dyes, wool pile, cotton warp and weft, approx. 12' x 18'. *Courtesy of Global Rug Corp./Woven Arts, Inc.* Estimated value $19,000.

New Chinese carpet. Inspired by old French Savonnerie carpet. Chrome dyes, wool pile, cotton warp and weft, approx. 8' 5" x 10'. *Courtesy of Renaissance Carpet & Tapestries, Inc.* Estimated value $12,500.

New Chinese carpet. Inspired by old French Savonnerie carpet. Chrome dyes, wool pile, cotton warp and weft, approx. 9' x 12' 9". *Courtesy of Renaissance Carpet & Tapestries, Inc.* Estimated value $17,000.

New Chinese carpet. Inspired by old French Savonnerie carpet. Chrome dyes, wool pile, cotton warp and weft, approx. 11' x 16'. *Courtesy of Renaissance Carpet & Tapestries, Inc.* Estimated value $26,000.

New Chinese carpet. Inspired by old French Savonnerie carpet. Chrome dyes, wool pile, cotton warp and weft, approx. 11' x 16'. *Courtesy of Renaissance Carpet & Tapestries, Inc.* Estimated value $26,000.

Above: New Chinese carpet. Inspired by old French Savonnerie carpet. Chrome dyes, wool pile, cotton warp and weft, approx. 14' x 24'. *Courtesy of Renaissance Carpet & Tapestries, Inc.* Estimated value $50,000.

Left: New Chinese carpet. Inspired by old French Savonnerie carpet. Chrome dyes, wool pile, cotton warp and weft, approx. 13' x 19'. *Courtesy of Renaissance Carpet & Tapestries, Inc.* Estimated value $37,000.

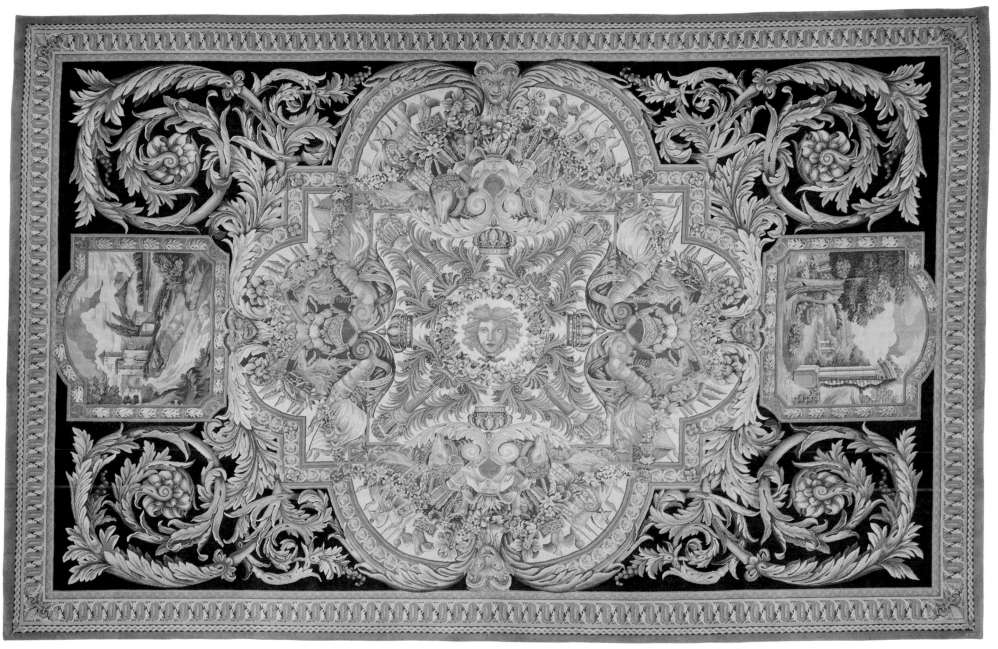

New Chinese carpet. Inspired by old French Savonnerie carpet. Chrome dyes, wool pile, cotton warp and weft, approx. 13' x 20'. *Courtesy of Renaissance Carpet & Tapestries, Inc.* Estimated value $39,000.

Kilims are the simplest flatweaves and consist of horizontal weft shoots in different colors and lengths that run back and forth across the long vertical warp threads. They differ from pile carpets because no small tufts of wool are looped around the warps and between the wefts.

A new kilim may be a better investment than a piled rug if one can find a fine quality, natural dyed, attractive example, preferably room-sized. The cost of the best will be less than piled weavings but still at least $30 a square foot at retail. Kilims are significantly underrated and unappreciated in the United States.

Because they usually wear out more quickly, there are far fewer good old flatweaves extant than knotted carpets. Old and rare kilims in good condition tend to be quite expensive and interesting new flatweaves are scarce. Turkey was the homeland of most of the great old kilims that are sought after in the trade. Fine antique Caucasian Shirvan and Persian Senneh flatweaves are also highly prized by rug dealers. Semi-antique Turkish Bessarabian-designed kilims, chemically washed and about forty years old, may be good buys if beautiful examples can be found in perfect condition, without repair or color run.

While flatweaves have the disadvantage of lacking the textural or tactile aesthetic of pile, they have many advantages over carpets. They are usually reversible and easy to manage, move, and store. They also have vivacious, and robust designs and colors. Some of the great antique examples have archaic designs that epitomize the tribal consciousness unfettered by Western taste. They are perhaps the most primordial weavings from the Middle East. Kilims wear well if properly cared for, require light vacuuming, and produce less dust than knotted rugs. They can be dry cleaned and are often more resistant to moths if the wool is not too greasy.

Most flatweaves are geometric because of the nature of the weave. Designs must be stepped or staggered in order for the piece to have a solid foundation. Changes in pattern or color often result in small slits or spaces between the warps. The slits are not flaws provided the weaving does not have so many as to become too delicate. Women who wear high heeled shoes should avoid kilims with too many slits. Lazy lines, or longer diagonal seams, are common to flatweaves and are not considered imperfections.

Soumaks are some of the most popular flatweaves with unusual stitching patterns. The soumak brocaded weave consists of colored weft yarns wrapped around groups of warp threads. The front side of the weaving has a different look and texture than the back of the textile. Antique Caucasian soumaks are

highly coveted and usually worn, painted, and costly, if in good condition. The best have rust, blue, ivory, green, and yellow vegetal dyes. Synthetically dyed and sun-bleached soumaks, around forty years old, are usually in excellent condition, but often contain hot orange, grey, pink, and brown colors. They are not very valuable and should retail for about $40 a foot. Many superb soumaks that closely approximate the colors, designs, and patina of important antique piled carpets are being made in China today.

The verneh or jijim is a flatweave with a plain weave foundation and brocading on the surface of the textile.

Aubussons have intricate, generally floral designs, and a complex, curvilinear, weft-faced weave. Like many kilims, the colored weft yarns are not woven entirely across the width of the textile. Aubussons have a more rounded weft structure than most rectilinear flatweaves. Unlike most kilims, Aubussons are not reversible. Needlepoints are easier to make because the craftsman simply embroiders the design drawn on a stretched cotton canvas foundation. The weaver uses a needle to push colored threads up and back down through the next hole in the mesh substructure. Old Aubussons and needlepoints are usually in rough condition because they were woven without pile.

Some tasteful and extraordinary needlepoints and Aubussons, floral or geometric, are being produced in China that precisely replicate very expensive antique pieces. Needlepoints sell for around $70 and Aubussons approximately $90 per square foot at retail. Both have the potential to retain value and perhaps one day every other apartment on Park Avenue will have one of these weavings on the floor. They have severely disturbed the antique Aubusson and needlepoint markets and some prominent old carpet dealers are beginning to carry them. Slight shape irregularity is not a serious imperfection and may reduce the rigidity of certain weavings. Although superb examples can be found with only a few colors, a lot of detail and many different colors are usually good qualities to look for in these contemporary pieces. Beautiful needlepoints often have Aubusson designs and are chemically washed to achieve an older appearance. The best Aubussons generally have very similar shades of color adjacent to one another and are exact copies of the original prototypes from the nineteenth century and earlier. They are often tightly packed with two different colored yarns twisted together to add depth to certain designs. They have a stronger construction and better investment potential than needlepoints.

Tapestries for the wall have more detailed and complicated designs than Aubussons. They usually have more slits than Aubussons, and contain many more shades of color. Tapestry designs have tremendous depth, subtlety, and definition. Tapestries, like Aubussons, are not reversible.

French and Flemish wall tapestries from from the nineteenth and early twentieth centuries used to be more prevalent in the trade, but are now quite rare. Many were woven with wool and silk. Antique French tapestries generally have light, open, and delicate designs, and are often horizontally shaped. Old Flemish tapestries normally have a dark, somber, Northern European sensibility, and are frequently verdure, or filled with trees and greenery. Tapestries that are delicate, somber, open, and verdure are generally categorized in the trade as "French or Flemish." Long threads on the back are usually, but not necessarily, a sign that the piece is hand-made. A tapestry must be closely examined because it is difficult to tell if it is a fragment. Attractive subject matter is very important, and horizontal or square shapes are generally preferred over vertical structures. Look for small, late-nineteenth century examples in clean condition. While expensive, repairs are normally quite successful. One must be knowledgeable before investing in earlier tapestries because most are fragments. They are very dearly priced.

New fine wall tapestries from China are frequently superb copies of rare and complete antique French and Flemish prototypes. They may be among the best investments on the market today, if well bought. Look for attractive subject matter and realistic human and animal representations in these high quality textiles. Some new tapestries have interlocked colored wefts and fewer slits than others. Slits do not affect a tapestry's value or collectibility.

New Turkish kilim or flatweave. Inspired by old Anatolian kilim. Vegetal dyes, colored wool wefts, plain wool warps, approx. 5' 1" x 7' 6". *Courtesy of Marian Miller.* Estimated value $1,800.

New Turkish kilim or flatweave. Inspired by old Anatolian kilim. Vegetal dyes, colored wool wefts, plain wool warps, approx. 5' 2" x 7' 5". *Courtesy of Marian Miller.* Estimated value $1,800.

New Turkish kilim or flatweave. Inspired by old Anatolian kilim. Vegetal dyes, colored wool wefts, plain wool warps, approx. 5' 11" x 8'. *Courtesy of Marian Miller*. Estimated value $2,400.

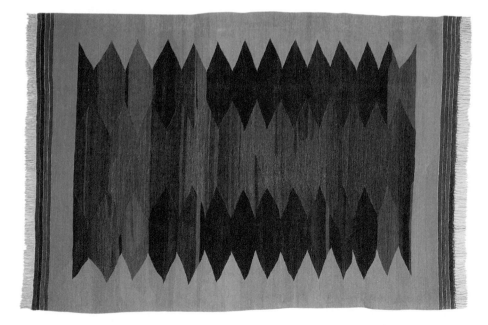

Above: New Turkish kilim or flatweave. Inspired by old Anatolian kilim. Vegetal dyes, colored wool wefts, plain wool warps, approx. 5' 10" x 8' 4". *Courtesy of Marian Miller*. Estimated value $2,400.
Right: New Turkish kilim or flatweave. Inspired by old Anatolian kilim. Vegetal dyes, colored wool wefts, plain wool warps, approx. 6' 3" x 9' 4". *Courtesy of Marian Miller*. Estimated value $2,600.

New Turkish kilim or flatweave. Woven with minimal Western guidance. Vegetal dyes, curved colored wool wefts, plain wool warps, approx. 9' 4" x 12' 6". *Courtesy of Woven Legends, Inc./Michaelian & Kohlberg, Inc.* Estimated value $3,600.

New Turkish kilim or flatweave. Inspired by old Thracian kilim. Vegetal dyes, colored wool wefts, plain wool warps, approx. 12' x 13'. *Courtesy of Woven Legends, Inc./ Michaelian & Kohlberg, Inc.* Estimated value $5,000.

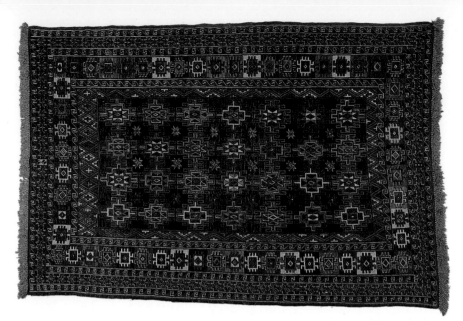

New Afghanistan soumak flatweave. Inspired by Caucasian designs, woven with minimal Western guidance. Vegetal dyes, colored wool wefts wrapped around groups of plain wool warps, approx. 5' x 8'. *Courtesy of Yayla Tribal Rugs.* Estimated value $1,200.

New Chinese soumak flatweave. Inspired by old Indian Agra carpet. Chrome and vegetal dyes, colored wool wefts wrapped around groups of plain cotton warps, approx. 5' 10" x 8' 10". *Courtesy of Nourison Rug Corp.* Estimated value $1,400.

New Chinese soumak flatweave. Inspired by old Turkish Oushak carpet. Chrome and vegetal dyes, colored wool wefts wrapped around groups of plain cotton warps, approx. 7' 10" x 9' 10". *Courtesy of Nourison Rug Corp.* Estimated value $2,100.

New Chinese soumak flatweave. Inspired by old Persian Baktiari carpet. Chrome and vegetal dyes, colored wool wefts wrapped around groups of plain cotton warps, approx. 5' 10" x 8' 10". *Courtesy of Nourison Rug Corp.* Estimated value $1,400.

New Chinese soumak flatweave. Inspired by old Indian Agra carpet. Chrome and vegetal dyes, colored wool wefts wrapped around groups of plain cotton warps, approx. 7' 10" x 9' 10". *Courtesy of Nourison Rug Corp.* Estimated value $2,100.

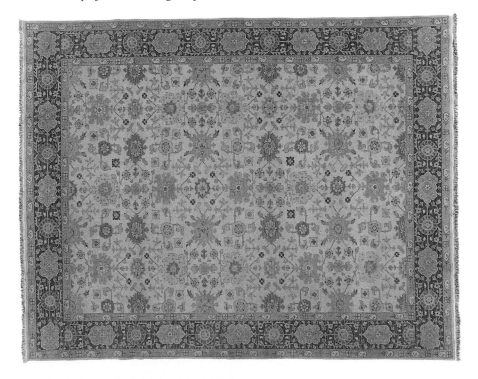

New Chinese soumak flatweave. Inspired by old Indian Agra carpet. Chrome and vegetal dyes, colored wool wefts wrapped around groups of plain cotton warps, approx. 7' 10" x 9' 10". *Courtesy of Nourison Rug Corp.* Estimated value $3,400.

New Chinese soumak flatweave. Inspired by old Persian Sultanabad carpet. Chrome and vegetal dyes, colored wool wefts wrapped around groups of plain cotton warps, approx. 7' 10" x 9' 10". *Courtesy of Nourison Rug Corp.* Estimated value $3,400.

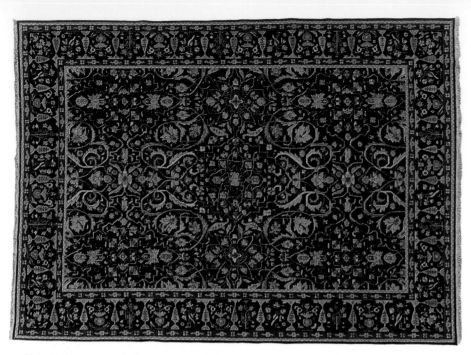

New Chinese soumak flatweave. Inspired by old Persian Lavar Kerman carpet. Chrome and vegetal dyes, colored wool wefts wrapped around groups of plain cotton warps, approx. 8' 10" x 11' 10". *Courtesy of Nourison Rug Corp*. Estimated value $4,400.

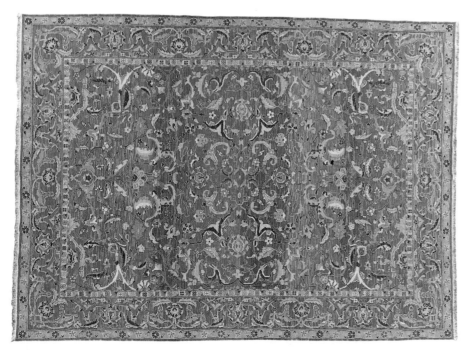

Old Caucasian soumak flatweave. Vegetal dyes, colored wool wefts wrapped around groups of plain wool warps, approx. 3' 4" x 6' 3". Partially oxidized black wool, slight wear, very good condition, c. 1880. *Courtesy of Christie's, Inc.* Estimated value $5,000.

New Chinese soumak flatweave. Inspired by old Persian Kerman carpet. Chrome and vegetal dyes, colored wool wefts wrapped around groups of plain cotton warps, approx. 8' 10" x 11' 10". *Courtesy of Nourison Rug Corp*. Estimated value $4,400.

Old Caucasian soumak flatweave. Dragon design. Vegetal dyes, colored wool wefts wrapped around groups of plain cotton warps, approx. 9' 6" x 12' 6". Small repair on end, very good condition, c. 1890. *Courtesy of Kamali Oriental Rugs*. Estimated value $20,000.

Old Caucasian verneh flatweave. Sileh design. Vegetal dyes, colored wool brocading, red wool foundation, approx. 6' 8" x 11'. Excellent condition, c. 1900. *Courtesy of Christie's, Inc.* Estimated value $12,000.

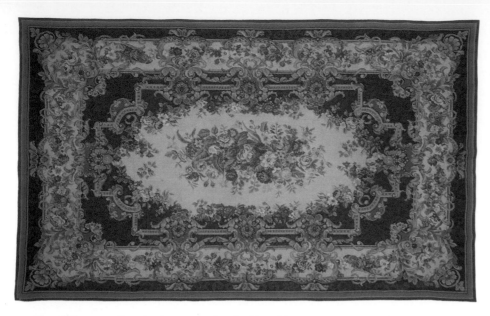

New Chinese needlepoint flatweave. Inspired by old French Aubusson. Chrome dyes, colored wool embroidery, cotton meshed canvas foundation, approx. 6' x 9'. *Courtesy of Samad Brothers, Inc.* Estimated value $2,400.

New Chinese needlepoint flatweave. Inspired by old French Aubusson. Chrome dyes, colored wool embroidery, cotton meshed canvas foundation, approx. 8' x 10'. *Courtesy of Samad Brothers, Inc.* Estimated value $3,600.

New Chinese needlepoint flatweave. Inspired by old French textile. Chrome dyes, colored wool embroidery, cotton meshed canvas foundation, approx. 8' x 10'. *Courtesy of Samad Brothers, Inc.* Estimated value $3,600.

New Chinese needlepoint flatweave. Inspired by old Flemish tapestry. Chrome dyes, colored wool embroidery, cotton meshed canvas foundation, approx. 8' x 11'. *Courtesy of Michaelian & Kohlberg, Inc.* Estimated value $3,800.

New Chinese needlepoint flatweave. Inspired by old English needlepoint. Chrome dyes, colored wool embroidery, cotton meshed canvas foundation, approx. 7' x 13'. *Courtesy of Michaelian & Kohlberg, Inc.* Estimated value $3,900.

New Chinese needlepoint flatweave. Inspired by old French needlepoint. Chrome dyes, colored wool embroidery, cotton meshed canvas foundation, approx. 8' x 10'. *Courtesy of Michaelian & Kohlberg, Inc.* Estimated value $3,400.

New Chinese needlepoint flatweave. Western contemporary design. Chrome dyes, colored wool embroidery, cotton meshed canvas foundation, approx. 8' x 10'. *Courtesy of Peel & Company, Inc.* Estimated value $3,200.

New Chinese needlepoint flatweave. Inspired by old French Aubusson. Chrome dyes, colored wool embroidery, cotton meshed canvas foundation, approx. 8' x 10'. *Courtesy of Peel & Company, Inc.* Estimated value $3,200.

New Chinese needlepoint flatweave. Western contemporary design. Chrome dyes, colored wool embroidery, cotton meshed canvas foundation, approx. 8' x 10'. *Courtesy of Peel & Company, Inc.* Estimated value $3,200.

New Chinese needlepoint flatweave. Western contemporary design. Chrome dyes, colored wool embroidery, cotton meshed canvas foundation, approx. 8' x 10'. *Courtesy of Peel & Company, Inc.* Estimated value $3,200.

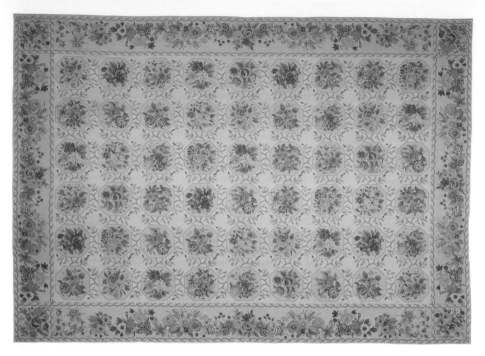

New Chinese needlepoint flatweave. Inspired by old English needlepoint. Chrome dyes, colored wool embroidery, cotton meshed canvas foundation, approx. 9' x 12'. *Courtesy of Aminco, Inc.* Estimated value $2,700.

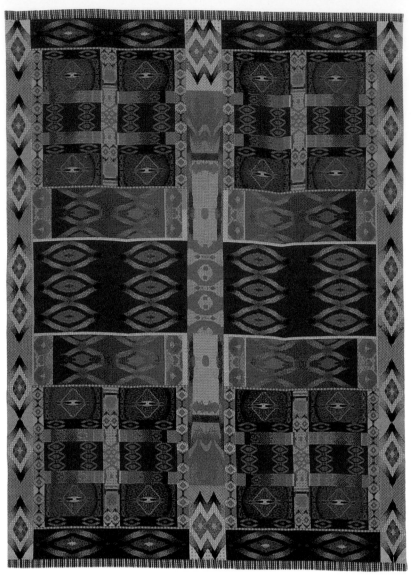

New Chinese needlepoint flatweave. Western contemporary design created by Tim Van Campen. Chrome dyes, colored wool embroidery, cotton meshed canvas foundation, approx. 7' x 10'. *Courtesy of Michaelian & Kohlberg, Inc.* Estimated value $3,000.

New Chinese needlepoint flatweave. Inspired by old French Aubusson. Chrome dyes, colored wool embroidery, cotton meshed canvas foundation, approx. 9' x 12'. *Courtesy of Aminco. Inc.* Estimated value $2,700.

New Chinese needlepoint flatweave. Western contemporary design created by Tim Van Campen. Chrome dyes, colored wool embroidery, cotton meshed canvas foundation, approx. 8' x 10'. *Courtesy of Michaelian & Kohlberg, Inc.* Estimated value $3,400.

Above: New Chinese Aubusson flatweave. Inspired by old French Aubusson. Chrome dyes, colored wool wefts, plain cotton warps, approx. 7' 10" x 10'. *Courtesy of Renaissance Carpet & Tapestries, Inc.* Estimated value $6,300.
Left: New Chinese Aubusson flatweave. Inspired by old French Aubusson. Chrome dyes, colored wool wefts, plain cotton warps, approx. 7' x 10'. *Courtesy of Michaelian & Kohlberg, Inc.* Estimated value $3,700.

New Chinese Aubusson flatweave. Inspired by old French Aubusson. Chrome dyes, colored wool wefts, plain cotton warps, approx. 8' x 10'. *Courtesy of Harounian Rugs International Co.* Estimated value $4,800.

New Chinese Aubusson flatweave. Inspired by old French Aubusson. Chrome dyes, colored wool wefts, plain cotton warps, approx. 8' x 10'. *Courtesy of Harounian Rugs International Co.* Estimated value $4,800.

New Chinese Aubusson flatweave. Inspired by old European floral design. Chrome dyes, colored wool wefts, plain cotton warps, approx. 8' x 10'. *Courtesy of Michaelian & Kohlberg, Inc.* Estimated value $4,200.

New Chinese Aubusson flatweave. Western contemporary design. Chrome dyes, colored wool wefts, plain cotton warps, approx. 8' x 10'. *Courtesy of Peel & Company, Inc.* Estimated value $5,600.

New Chinese Aubusson flatweave. Inspired by old French Aubusson. Chrome dyes, colored wool wefts, plain cotton warps, approx. 11' x 13' 6". *Courtesy of Michaelian & Kohlberg, Inc.* Estimated value $7,800.

New Chinese Aubusson flatweave. Inspired by old French Aubusson. Chrome dyes, colored wool wefts, plain cotton warps, approx. 9' x 9'. *Courtesy of Michaelian & Kohlberg, Inc.* Estimated value $4,300.

New Chinese Aubusson flatweave. Inspired by old French Aubusson. Chrome dyes, colored wool wefts, plain cotton warps, approx. 10' x 10'. *Courtesy of Renaissance Carpet & Tapestries, Inc.* Estimated value $8,000.

New Chinese Aubusson flatweave. Inspired by old Bessarabian kilim. Chrome dyes, colored wool wefts, plain cotton warps, approx. 9' x 12'. *Courtesy of French Accents Rugs & Tapestries, Inc.* Estimated value $6,800.

New Chinese Aubusson flatweave. Inspired by old French Aubusson. Chrome dyes, colored wool wefts, plain cotton warps, approx. 9' x 12'. *Courtesy of French Accents Rugs & Tapestries, Inc.* Estimated value $6,800.

New Chinese Aubusson flatweave. Inspired by old French Aubusson. Chrome dyes, colored wool wefts, plain cotton warps, approx. 9' x 12'. *Courtesy of French Accents Rugs & Tapestries, Inc.* Estimated value $6,800.

New Chinese Aubusson flatweave. Inspired by old French Aubusson. Chrome dyes, colored wool wefts, plain cotton warps, approx. 9' x 12'. *Courtesy of French Accents Rugs & Tapestries, Inc.* Estimated value $6,800.

New Chinese Aubusson flatweave. Inspired by old French Aubusson. Chrome dyes, colored wool wefts, plain cotton warps, approx. 9' x 12'. *Courtesy of Renaissance Carpet & Tapestries, Inc.* Estimated value $8,500.

New Chinese Aubusson flatweave. Inspired by old French Aubusson. Chrome dyes, colored wool wefts, plain cotton warps, approx. 10' x 12'. *Courtesy of French Accents Rugs & Tapestries, Inc.* Estimated value $7,500.

New Chinese Aubusson flatweave. Inspired by old French Aubusson. Chrome dyes, colored wool wefts, plain cotton warps, approx. 10' x 14'. *Courtesy of Renaissance Carpet & Tapestries, Inc.* Estimated value $11,000.

New Chinese Aubusson flatweave. Inspired by old French Aubusson. Chrome dyes, colored wool wefts, plain cotton warps, approx. 10' x 14'. *Courtesy of Michaelian & Kohlberg, Inc.* Estimated value $7,400.

New Chinese Aubusson flatweave. Inspired by old French Aubusson. Chrome dyes, colored wool wefts, plain cotton warps, approx. 10' x 14'. *Courtesy of Renaissance Carpet & Tapestries, Inc.* Estimated value $11,000.

New Chinese Aubusson flatweave. Inspired by old French Aubusson. Chrome dyes, colored wool wefts, plain cotton warps, approx. 10' x 14'. *Courtesy of Renaissance Carpet & Tapestries, Inc.* Estimated value $11,000.

New Chinese Aubusson flatweave. Inspired by old French Aubusson. Chrome dyes, colored wool wefts, plain cotton warps, approx. 10' x 14'. *Courtesy of Renaissance Carpet & Tapestries, Inc.* Estimated value $11,000.

Old French Aubusson flatweave. Vegetal dyes, colored wool wefts, plain cotton warps, approx. 4' 10" x 13'. Excellent condition, c. 1890. *Courtesy of Eliko Antique & Decorative Rugs.* Estimated value $12,500.

New Chinese Aubusson flatweave. Inspired by old French Aubusson. Chrome dyes, colored wool wefts, plain cotton warps, approx. 13' x 18'. *Courtesy of French Accents Rugs & Tapestries, Inc.* Estimated value 14,500.

Old French Aubusson flatweave. Vegetal dyes, colored wool wefts, plain cotton warps, approx. 9' x 12'. Small stains, very good condition, c. 1890. *Courtesy of Abraham Moheban & Son.* Estimated value $20,000.

Old French Aubusson flatweave. Vegetal dyes, colored wool wefts, plain cotton warps, approx. 11' x 13' 9". Excellent condition, c. 1900. *Courtesy of Christie's, Inc.* Estimated value $35,000.

Old French Aubusson flatweave. Vegetal dyes, colored wool wefts, plain cotton warps, approx. 11' x 14' 11". Minor stains, excellent condition, c. 1890. *Courtesy of Christie's, Inc.* Estimated value 30,000.

Old French Aubusson flatweave. Vegetal dyes, colored wool wefts, plain cotton warps, approx. 16' x 20'. Excellent condition, c. 1890. *Courtesy of Iraj Fine Oriental Rugs, Inc.* Estimated value $110,000.

New Chinese tapestry. Inspired by old Flemish verdure tapestry. Chrome dyes, colored wool and silk slit-woven wefts, plain wool warps, approx. 4' x 6'. *Courtesy of French Accents Rugs & Tapestries, Inc.* Estimated value $4000.

New Chinese tapestry. Inspired by old Flemish verdure tapestry. Chrome dyes, colored wool and silk slit-woven wefts, plain wool warps, approx. 7' x 7' 4". *Courtesy of French Accents Rugs & Tapestries, Inc.* Estimated value $6300.

New Chinese tapestry. Inspired by old French tapestry. Chrome dyes, colored wool and silk interlocked wefts, plain cotton warps, approx. 7' x 12'. *Courtesy of Renaissance Carpet & Tapestries, Inc.* Estimated value $10,000.

New Chinese tapestry. Inspired by old French tapestry. Chrome dyes, colored wool and silk slit-woven wefts, plain wool warps, approx. 5' 6" x 7' 4". *Courtesy of French Accents Rugs & Tapestries, Inc.* Estimated value $7,300.

New Chinese tapestry. Inspired by old French gothic or medieval millefleurs tapestry. Chrome dyes, colored wool and silk interlocked wefts, plain cotton warps, approx. 5' 7" x 8' 8". *Courtesy of Renaissance Carpet & Tapestries, Inc.* Estimated value $5,800.

Old Flemish tapestry. Vegetal dyes, colored wool and silk wefts, plain wool warps, approx. 7' x 16'. Fragment, excellent condition, c. 1675. *Courtesy of Iraj Fine Oriental Rugs, Inc.* Estimated value $45,000.

Machine-made Rugs

There is a lot of creativity today in machine-made rugs. Some are of such high quality that they cost almost as much as handmade pieces. A small number of the very best machine-made carpets may even retain value over time. Old Karastans in excellent condition are still being bought by a few old rug dealers, and some of the best new Couristans from Belgium, that retail for about $25 per square foot, could be collectible.

There are factories in the United States and Belgium that are doing serious work and producing beautiful pieces, treated for easy care and durability. They have softer backs today that almost feel like handmade carpets and are often guaranteed for many years. Look for unusual examples with wool and cotton rather than synthetic fibers. The best pieces often have good detail and similar complementary shades of color. Designs should not be too mechanical and colors should closely approximate the hues found in antique weavings. Canary yellows, pistachio greens, corals, and other pastel colors are as desirable in machine-made as they are in hand-woven rugs. Some machine-made carpets are very similar to great old pieces and rival hand-made copies in faithfully reproducing color, texture, and design.

Machine-made rugs sometimes have fuzzy backs and the weave is perfectly symmetrical and mechanical. The abrashes, or changes in the values of individual colors, are often either too evenly balanced or glaringly unbalanced, and the designs generally lack the high definition of hand-made carpets. The knots on the back of machine-made rugs are woven in absolutely straight, frequently wavy lines that never vary from row to row.

Hand-made weavings will always have irregularities if one examines the back closely. The wefts, or threads that are woven horizontally across the carpet, will ordinarily vary only slightly from one row to another. Even the new rugs from India, Pakistan, and China that are quite symmetrical are not as rigidly ordered as machine-made pieces.

Hand-tufted and gun-punched carpets often have latex backings that prevent knots from being pulled out of the foundation. These rugs usually have a canvas covering on the back which indicates that the knots are fused or glued into the foundation rather than power-loomed through the substructure. The carpets are a little delicate and should be carefully cleaned.

Antique nineteenth century power-loomed rugs from the cities of Axminister and Wilton in England may be very valuable today. Some were woven in strips with the pile intermeshed with the foundation, and others were woven in one piece with a looped pile similar to hand-made carpets. They are rarely found in the trade.

Antique American machine-made rugs known as Wiltons were woven in Art Deco, Art Nouveau, or Oriental-style designs. The Art Deco and Art Nouveau carpets are more valuable than the copies of classical Persian rugs. Old Wiltons were loomed in strips of varying lengths, up to around three feet wide. The seamed areas where the strips were sewn together should preferably be flat, and only slightly visible. Runners were often made to order in different lengths and bound at the edges and ends. Antique American Wiltons are very durable and may be good investments if attractive examples can be found, without stains or significant wear, and bought at the right price. A beautiful 9 x 12 Art Nouveau piece should cost about $6,000 at retail. They are becoming more coveted in recent years.

New Belgian machine-made carpet. Inspired by old Persian Serape carpet. Chrome dyes, wool pile, cotton foundation, approx. 5' 9" x 6' 3". *Courtesy of Louis De Poortere.* Estimated value $900.

New Belgian machine-made carpet. Inspired by old Persian Bakshaiash carpet. Cypress and weeping willow tree designs. Chrome dyes, wool pile, cotton foundation, approx. 5' 7" x 7' 7". *Courtesy of Karastan.* Estimated value $1,100.

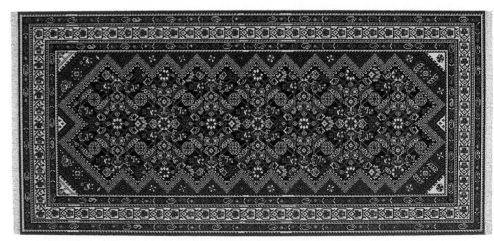

New Belgian machine-made carpet. Inspired by old Persian Malayer carpet. Chrome dyes, wool pile, cotton foundation, approx. 3' x 6' 3". *Courtesy of Louis De Poortere.* Estimated value $350.

New Belgian machine-made carpet. Inspired by old Caucasian soumak flatweave. Chrome dyes, wool pile, cotton foundation, approx. 6' x 9'. *Courtesy of Louis De Poortere.* Estimated value $900.

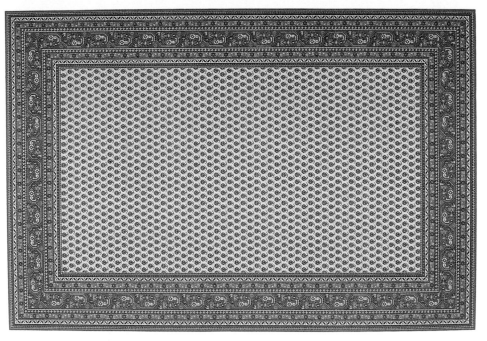

New Belgian machine-made carpet. Inspired by old Persian Serraband carpet. Mir-i boteh design. Chrome dyes, wool pile, cotton foundation, approx. 6' x 9'. *Courtesy of Louis De Poortere.* Estimated value $500.

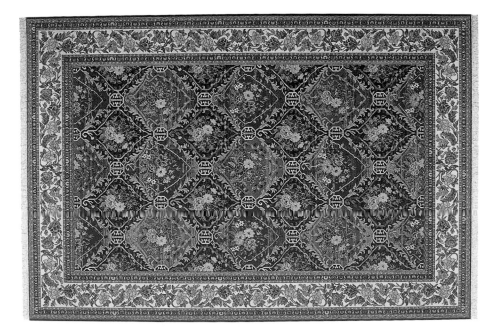

New Belgian machine-made carpet. Inspired by old Persian Baktiari carpet. Chrome dyes, wool pile, cotton foundation, approx. 6' x 9'. *Courtesy of Louis De Poortere.* Estimated value $1,100.

New American machine-made carpet. Inspired by old Persian Kurdish carpet. Chrome dyes, wool pile, cotton foundation, approx. 5' 8" x 8' 11". *Courtesy of Karastan.* Estimated value $2,000.

New American machine-made carpet. Inspired by old Persian Kerman Vase carpet. Chrome dyes, wool pile, cotton foundation, approx. 5' 8" x 8' 11". *Courtesy of Karastan.* Estimated value $2,000.

New Belgian machine-made carpet. Inspired by old Persian Sarouk carpet. Chrome dyes, wool pile, cotton foundation, approx. 5' 5" x 8' 6". *Courtesy of Karastan.* Estimated value $1,100.

New Belgian machine-made carpet. Inspired by old Persian Kashan carpet. Chrome dyes, wool pile, cotton foundation, approx. 5' 5" x 8' 6". *Courtesy of Karastan.* Estimated value $1,400.

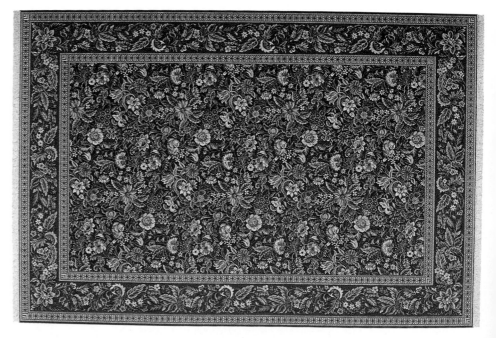

New Belgian machine-made carpet. Inspired by old European floral designs. Chrome dyes, wool pile, cotton foundation, approx. 6' x 9'. *Courtesy of Louis De Poortere.* Estimated value $1,100.

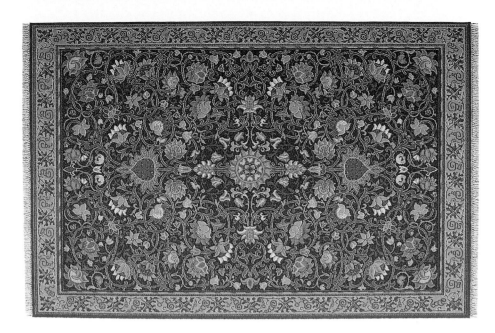

New Belgian machine-made carpet. Inspired by old English Arts and Crafts carpet. Chrome dyes, wool pile, cotton foundation, approx. 6' x 9'. *Courtesy of Louis De Poortere.* Estimated value $1,400.

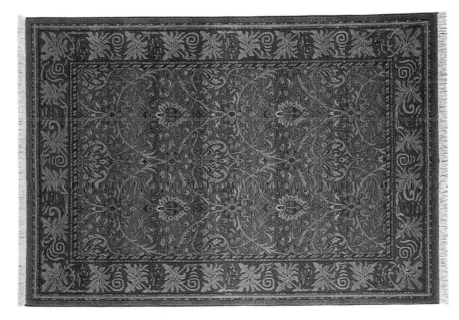

New Belgian machine-made carpet. Inspired by old oriental carpet. Chrome dyes, wool pile, cotton foundation, approx. 5' 7" x 8' 3". *Courtesy of Couristan, Inc.* Estimated value $1,400.

New Belgian machine-made carpet. Inspired by old oriental carpet. Chrome dyes, wool pile, cotton foundation, approx. 5' 7" x 8' 3". *Courtesy of Couristan, Inc.* Estimated value $1,400.

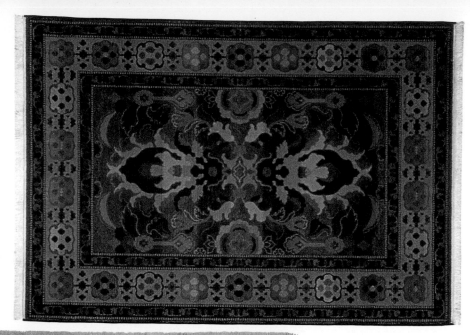

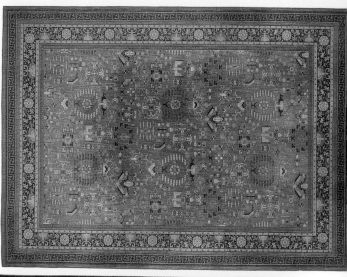

Old American Wilton machine-made carpet. Chinese-inspired Art Deco design. Synthetic dyes, wool pile, cotton foundation, approx. 9' x 12'. Slight wear, uneven fading, small stains, good condition, c. 1920. *Courtesy of Alice's Antiques.* Estimated value $6,000.

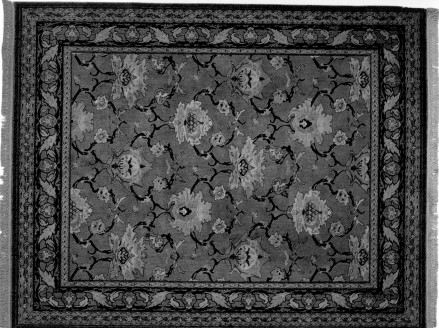

New Belgian machine-made carpet. Inspired by old oriental carpet. Chrome dyes, wool pile, cotton foundation, approx. 5' 7" x 8' 3". *Courtesy of Couristan, Inc.* Estimated value $1,400.

Old American Wilton machine-made carpet. Art Nouveau bird of paradise design. Synthetic dyes, wool pile, cotton foundation, approx. 9' x 12'. Excellent condition, c. 1920. *Courtesy of Alice's Antiques.* Estimated value $7,500.

Above: Old American Wilton machine-made carpet. Art Nouveau design. Synthetic dyes, wool pile, cotton foundation, approx. 8' x 10'. Loss of pile in corner, stains, good condition, c. 1920. *Courtesy of Alice's Antiques.* Estimated value $7,000.

Below: Old American Wilton machine-made carpet. Art Deco design. Synthetic dyes, wool pile, cotton foundation, approx. 2' x 11'. Wear in a few areas and selvedge, good condition, c. 1920. *Courtesy of Alice's Antiques.* Estimated value $2,000.

New Programmed Rugs

Many new carpets are programmed. This means that a particular piece is available in various sizes and may be ordered from the retailer's samples. The sizes are usually indicated on the tag but one should ask the salesman to check the computer to see if the rug is still in production. Some producers have more extensive and complete programs than others, and more sizes constantly available in their warehouses. Other manufacturers may have continuity of production, but more limited programming, with fewer sizes obtainable at a given time.

Programming of new carpets was a great innovation that was developed about twenty years ago. It obviated the wholesaler or importer from having to consign hundreds of rugs to retailers. In the old days, carpets would have to be trucked back and forth between the supplier and retailer at great expense, and pieces would often get dirty. Now, the customer simply orders a fresh piece from the sample, and the retailer secures the rug from the wholesaler. The carpet remains in a warehouse until purchased by the client.

Normally, it does not take more than a few weeks to order a rug, but it may be a shade or two lighter or darker than the sample. Slight color variation should be acceptable as dye lots and yarns vary. However, if the carpet ordered is several shades different from the sample, it should probably be rejected.

Programmed rugs have improved so much in recent years that most are as collectible as one-of-a-kind new carpets. Many of the finest formal, floral, hand-made rugs from India, Pakistan, and China as well as machine-made carpets are programmed. More and more informal or geometric hand-made weavings are being programmed today.

The Future of New Rugs

The question of which contemporary carpets have antique potential is difficult to answer because every dealer has a different idea on the subject.

The first group of dealers believes that no new weavings other than perhaps the finest Iranian or Persian rugs have the possibility of retaining significant value. These dealers contend that the old carpet trade will soon be over in the United States unless the ban on imported goods from Iran is lifted. They maintain that as long as the production of Indian, Pakistani, and Chinese rugs remains high, and the market is saturated, almost all new pieces imported into this country should be considered commodities only, with little investment potential.

A second group claims that only the finest new carpets, kilims, Aubussons, and needlepoints with very high knot counts, from any country, will hold value. Many old rug dealers fall into this camp.

A third group is a little more liberal and adds a few more types with medium and coarser weaves such as Egyptian, Turkish village, Tibetan, and other extremely attractive Indian, Pakistani, and Chinese pieces. These dealers believe that because labor is cheap in the East, materials are generally more important determinents of quality than knot count. They contend that a fine weave with poor wool or dyes is far worse than a coarse weave with better materials. The carpets should be interesting and beautiful when viewed from five to ten feet away, which is the proper distance for addressing a rug, and, if possible, up close. All should have the finest wool, dyes, and workmanship with no corners cut in order to remain extant and retain value. If any aspect of production is second grade, which is sometimes the case, the piece will most likely not be re-salable. Famous and superlative innovators, who develop great designs and maintain the highest standards of excellence in every aspect of production, are more likely to create antiques of the future than pathbreakers who sacrifice quality in quest of the dollar. Excellent, lanolin-rich New Zealand wool that is poorly dyed will not hold color over time. Rugs must be kept in mint condition as repair beyond fringes and selvedges will probably not be warranted in the forseeable future. Brand recognition characteristic of enduring contemporary classics will help retain value as well. Exact reproductions of the best antique pieces may be collectible, but they must be almost indistinguishable from the originals. New piled carpets with antique potential should be rather expensive and have a fair retail price of over $60 a square foot.

A fourth, relatively small, group of new rug dealers believes all hand-made weavings that are reasonably well constructed will retain value because cheap labor is diminishing worldwide. Carpet weavers in India, Pakistan, China, and elsewhere are gradually switching to better jobs that pay more, and are becoming security guards, apple vendors, and doormen. As the information age and capitalism reduce the number of people interested in weaving, the value of rugs will rise. In addition, this group maintains that while Iranian carpets are generally the best, Indian, Pakistani, and Chinese rugs are normally better values at lower price points. They believe that there is not much difference between Iranian and Indian weavings because all areas of the Middle East borrowed from one another, were merged centuries ago, and are sister countries. There are some new Indian carpets that are almost indistinguishable from contemporary Tibetan rugs, and many modern Pakistani pieces that look exactly like new Afghan weavings. It is also hard to tell the difference between certain new, natural-dyed Turkish carpets and kilims and some Chinese copies. Since there are so many modern productions from all different countries no one will be able to determine where the pieces were made in the future. Therefore, this group of predominantly new rug importers concludes that provenance may be less significant in future rug evaluations.

A fifth group says color is the paramount variable in predicting future salability. These dealers contend that most old carpets have primarily decorative value; therefore, new rugs will also be mainly sought after as room embellishments. Because of the ever-growing strength of the decorator trade, there will always be a need for strikingly beautiful carpets with superb color combinations for the designers of the future. The fact that the antique Oushak, a coarsely woven and usually worn piece, is so highly esteemed in the trade for its color, lends credence to this view.

Regardless of whether one believes almost all new rugs are commodities or objects of intrinsic worth, the old carpet trade is in disarray and depression because of this renaissance of contemporary weavings. There was a time in the past when old rather than new rugs were better values because of superior weave, dyes, and craftsmanship. About forty years ago many people in the United States were throwing out valuable, room-sized rugs in order to buy broadloom carpets. Good antique pieces that were quite cheap thirty years ago are scarcer, and therefore dearer, than new carpets today. One positive consequence of this price reversal is that many people are now taking better care of their old rugs.

Old Rugs

Each town has a distinctive knot shape that is recognized by viewing the back of the carpet. Every locale will also have certain designs and colors associated with it. Occasionally a rug may have a design from one area and a knot structure from another. These so-called "bastard" carpets are generally not as valuable as those which have a clearly recognizable provenance. Some of the best old weavings from Iran (Persia) were woven in the following towns or districts: Kerman, Kashan, Sarouk, Ferahan, Bidjar, and Tabriz. These are usually more curvilinear, floral, or formal than the equally coveted but more geometric northwest Persian Heriz, Serape, and Mahal or Sultanabad.

Some of the main tribal and village carpets found in the trade include the Kazak and Shirvan from the Caucasus, Kurdish, Shiraz, Qashqai, and Afshar from Iran, Yoruk from Turkey, Turkoman from Turkmenistan, and Afghan from Afghanistan. These are usually geometric and found in small scatter sizes, although Turkoman and Afghan main carpets may be 9 x 12 feet and larger. Good old Kazaks and finely woven Shirvans, with their bold and powerful designs, have gone up in price a great deal, but better buys may still be found in Kurdish pieces, a less expensive alternative to Caucasian rugs. One "hot," synthetic, fugitive, or watery dye in the rug indicates that it may be late, or woven after around 1900, and reduces the carpet's value as a collectible considerably. Tangerine is probably a good vegetal dye, but bright orange is generally a bad synthetic color when found in these weavings. The Qashqai is fine and highly esteemed, and the more coarsely woven Shiraz

and Afshar have become more prized in recent years. Yoruk tend to be rarer and dearer than Kurdish but are normally quite worn. Antique Turkoman rugs, with their varying shades of red and symmetrical repeat designs, are highly sought after by collectors and expensive, if all the colors are good and the piece is rare. They are probably the most popular carpets among collectors and their exact, mathematically precise repetition of the same motif made them arguably the consummate artistic achievement of weavers in migratory peasant cultures. Older Turkomans frequently have fairly large, dramatic, and delicately drawn motifs or guls floating on majestic open fields in endless repeat patterns. The designs of later Turkomans are often more dull, regimented, and cluttered. Very rare and important small Turkoman bagfaced rugs called chuvals and camel coverings known as asmalyks may have the highest square-foot value of all old carpets. Prices of antique tribal and village weavings vary considerably and are based upon age, rarity, beauty, character, and condition.

China produced many classic antique city or workshop rugs and had no tribal or village tradition. Old Pekings, as well as the more recent 1940s "Nichols," Art Deco, or Tientsin carpets, are highly sought after if attractive and well preserved. Old Pekings are rare and have a fairly short pile. They are usually found with beige, blue, and ivory colors and varying degrees of wear. "Nichols" Chinese rugs are thick and heavy with strong, stable synthetic dyes. They convey the mood of the Art Deco period with flowers, butterflies, and unusual colors such as black, pink, gold, and taupe. Although it is becoming more and more difficult, the "Nichols" can still be procured in excellent condition without stains. Such a "Nichols" in 9 x 12 might sell for about $15,000, whereas an old Peking in the same size with a few low spots is generally more expensive, or around $20,000, at retail.

Thick, coarsely woven Hamadans from Iran were produced in large quantities and imported to the United States for decades. While they are normally not highly regarded in the trade, attractive pieces are becoming harder to find. Gaudy examples should usually be avoided. Old, thin, and fine vegetally-dyed Hamadans can sometimes be purchased in very good condition at a reasonable price. The "Camel" Hamadan and related Serab rugs usually have beautiful dark taupe and straw-colored wool from sheep. They are coveted partly because of the warmth of the ivory, camel, and brown hues.

Antique Oushaks are highly sought after decorative carpets with soft pastel colors, silky wool, and limited palettes. They have a fairly broad weave and are often quite worn. If secured in good condition, with few areas devoid of pile, they fetch high prices today, particularly if the colors are beautiful and the character is appealing. The fair retail price for such a piece in 9 x 12 is usually around $20,000 and up. However, one bad color such as sharp mustard or "acid" green will lower the value significantly. The cost of these weavings significantly depends upon the degree of wear. Later Oushaks, about

50 years old, are often found with either garish red and blue, or camel, blue, and pink colors. The camel are better than the bright red and blue rugs and are more valuable.

Senneh carpets from Iran, usually in scatter sizes, can be exceptional, fine, and expensive. Some of the best Senneh rugs are extraordinarily fine and small sized with silk warps of various colors visible at the ends.

Persian Lavar Kerman carpets are generally quite fine, in full-field design, with large center medallions. They are about a hundred years old and have many flowers in blue, ivory, pink, and red. Unfortunately, these stunning pieces are usually worn, extensively refurbished and painted, and at best in fair condition. They are nonetheless very popular in the United States and Italy and can be recommended if bought in fairly good condition at the right price. They contain the rare and true deep red color that is normally found in old Indian pieces.

Later Kerman rugs, around seventy years old, are usually a good value if the weave is fine, the wool silky, and the condition excellent. They have a full-field design with many flowers and swirling arabesques. These Kermans have a style that is reminiscent of European needlepoints. The colors are typically crimson red, blue, pink, and ivory, and the fair retail price is about $20,000 for a 9 x 12 foot carpet in excellent condition with no low areas.

More recent Kermans, around forty years old, are finely woven with thick, plush pile, pastel colors, and center medallions. They were quite popular in the United States at one time but are not as fashionable today. These Kermans are becoming more rare but should still preferably be purchased only if the pile is perfect. The retail value is about $16,000 for a 9 x 12 carpet.

Antique Herizes, Serapes, and Mahals from Iran are highly coveted in the trade, but their prices have gone up in recent years. They are rarely found in excellent condition, and the vast majority are extensively touched up and repaired. A beautiful 9 x 12, in good condition, with few worn areas, is around $25,000 at retail. If the weaving is in very good to excellent condition and has fairly good character, the price may be about $35,000. Pieces with better character are even more expensive because they are more difficult to find. Mahals are less geometric than Herizes and Serapes and have a softer, more granular weave. They are therefore usually more worn. Older Mahals are normally called Sultanabads. Although the Heriz has a design and weave that is slightly different from the Serape, the term "Heriz" may be used to refer to both carpets. In general, designs in older Herizes, Serapes, and Mahals are delicate and large scaled, with more open space between motifs. Herizes and Serapes are the most popular antique geometric rugs in the United States and many dealers specialize in them. The Bakshaiash is an old, highly coveted, often candy cane-colored Heriz that may sometimes have a wool warp and weft.

Mohtesham and Manchester Kashans, also from Iran, are among the most revered traditional formal carpets and are rarely found in excellent condition. A Mohtesham is more valuable, but usually more worn, than a Manchester Kashan. A 9 x 12 Manchester in good condition, with no badly worn spots, should be around $25,000, and a Mohtesham considerably more at retail.

Antique Persian Hadji Jahlili Tabrizes with their medallions and beautiful soft beige, rust, and ivory colors are also highly prized, with prices comparable to the very best Herizes, Serapes, and Mahals. The Hadji Jahlili Tabriz was beautifully copied about eighty years ago in the Turkish city of Sivas. The price of old Sivas rugs, also esteemed for their soft colors, has risen dramatically in recent years. Frequently magnificant Ferahans, also called Ferahan Sarouks, with fairly saturated colors, and a little more detail in the design, have similar valuations, if attractive and in very good condition. Old Bidjars, also coveted, may cost about $20,000 or more for a sound and beautiful 9 x 12 foot carpet. They are strong, stiff, and wear like iron.

The real Agras are Indian rugs that may be extremely expensive and reach some of the highest prices in the trade. They are thick, heavy, and densely packed with a ribbed knot structure. Colors are often striking and deeply saturated. They are rarely seen in the trade in good condition and should not be confused with later Indian carpets sometimes called Amritsar or Agra. These are thin, fairly fine, pale and soft, and although their prices have risen tremendously in recent years, they are not as valuable as the real Agra.

Savonneries are among the most highly regarded antique rugs from Europe, and their prices can reach the stratosphere. They vary greatly in value and wool quality. Some of the best pieces that have survived are from the time of Napoleon. Certain more recent examples from Europe are not real Savonneries, and may be unexceptional, with coarse wool, and flat, uninteresting, color palettes. There are also some excellent copies, with some age and the finest wool, that are probably from China.

Many old English hand-made carpets from the cities of Axminister and Wilton compared favorably with contemporaneous Middle Eastern weavings, and are priceless today.

Antique Spanish carpets are especially rare and expensive even if they are quite worn. Some of the earliest examples extant had a unique weave that consisted of knots looped around single warps. These pieces sometimes had a family's coat of arms woven into the rug. More recent examples are at times methodical and derivative, and some, made to order for certain companies around twenty years ago, have little value.

Older Karabagh carpets from the Caucasus have the flavor of European Savonneries and needlepoints but contain more highly geometric and stylized floral forms. They usually have dark background colors and unusual shapes, such as wide, long, runners and gallery sizes known as kelligis. The kelligis measure about 5 x 10 to 7 x 20 feet. Desirable antique Karabaghs have highly decorative, earth-toned hues with black and various shades of beige and brown colored wool. Later Karabaghs frequently have strong, bright, and even garish colors, but are still highly coveted in the trade if in excellent condition. Prices of Karabaghs have risen in recent years because they are quite popular, and an attractive, semi-antique kellegi, around sixty years old, in excellent condition, normally retails for approximately $20,000.

Unusual or uncommon semi-antique rugs that cannot be categorized by experts may be highly desirable, if attractive and well-preserved.

Old Persian Afshar carpet. Vegetal dyes, wool pile, warp, and weft, approx. 4' 4" x 5' 4". Excellent condition, c. 1920. *Courtesy of Christie's, Inc.* Estimated value $3,000.

Old Turkish Kirshehir carpet. Prayer design. Vegetal dyes, wool pile, warp, and weft, approx. 3' 3" x 4' 5". Loss of pile in three corners and ends, moderate, even wear, good condition, c. 1900. *Courtesy of John Batki.* Estimated value $4,500.

Old Persian Bakshaiash carpet. Vegetal dyes, wool pile, cotton warp and weft, approx. 4' 4" x 6' 5". Loss of pile on end, moderate wear, small repairs, good condition, c. 1900. *Courtesy of Abraham Moheban & Son.* Estimated value $3,500.

Old Turkmenistan Beshir carpet. Vegetal dyes, wool pile, warp, and weft, approx. 3' 6" x 6' 6". Heavy, even wear, repairs, fair condition, c. 1880. *Courtesy of Christie's, Inc.* Estimated value $4,000.

Old Turkmenistan Chodor carpet. Vegetal dyes, wool pile, warp, and weft, approx. 4' 1" x 5' 4". Slight loss of pile on selvedges and ends, moderate, even wear, good condition, c. 1900. *Courtesy of Christie's, Inc.* Estimated value $6,000.

Old Turkmenistan Beshir carpet. Vegetal dyes, wool pile, warp, and weft, approx. 5' x 9' 5". Rewoven end, heavy, even wear, repairs, fair condition, c. 1890. *Courtesy of Christie's, Inc.* Estimated value $4,000.

Old Turkish Bergama carpet. Vegetal dyes, wool pile, warp, and weft, approx. 6' 6" x 6' 10". Moderate wear, extensive repairs on sides and ends, other small repairs, fair condition, c. 1890. *Courtesy of Christie's, Inc.* Estimated value $7,000.

Old Caucasian Lori Pembak Kazak carpet. Vegetal dyes, wool pile, warp, and weft, approx. 5' 10" x 7' 7". Slight loss of pile on end and corner, excellent condition, c. 1900. *Courtesy of Christie's, Inc.* Estimated value $8,000.

Old Turkmenistan Tekke carpet. Vegetal dyes, wool pile, warp, and weft, approx. 6' 1" x 9' 5". Small slits and holes, very good condition, c. 1890. *Courtesy of Christie's, Inc.* Estimated value $15,000.

Old Caucasian Sewan Kazak carpet. Vegetal dyes, wool pile, warp, and weft, approx. 5' x 8'. Slight loss of pile in corners and end, light, even wear, good condition, c. 1910. *Courtesy of Abraham Moheban & Son.* Estimated value $15,000.

Old Caucasian Kazak carpet. Vegetal dyes, wool pile, warp, and weft, approx. 5' x 8' 1". Slight loss of pile on end, moderate wear, repairs, good condition, c. 1900. *Courtesy of Christie's, Inc.* Estimated value $5,000.

Old Caucasian Kazak carpet. Vegetal dyes, wool pile, warp, and weft, approx. 6' x 9' 10". Moderate wear, repairs, good condition, c. 1900. *Courtesy of Eliko Antique & Decorative Rugs.* Estimated value $22,000.

Old Persian Baktiari carpet. Vegetal dyes, wool pile, cotton warp and weft, approx. 6' 10" x 10' 4". Excellent condition, c. 1930. *Courtesy of Kamali Oriental Rugs.* Estimated value $12,000.

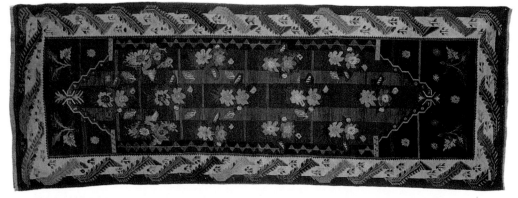

Old Turkish Melas carpet. Vegetal dyes, wool pile, warp, and weft, approx. 3' 4" x 8' 11". Partially oxidized black wool, even wear, good condition, c. 1900. *Courtesy of Abraham Moheban & Son.* Estimated value $6,000.

Old Persian "Camel" Hamadan carpet. Vegetal dyes, wool pile, cotton warp and weft, approx. 10' 5" x 13' 10". Moderate wear, extensive old repairs, fair condition, c. 1900. *Courtesy of Kamali Oriental Rugs.* Estimated value $27,000.

Old Caucasian
Shirvan carpet.
Probably vegetal
dyes, wool pile, warp,
and weft, approx. 2'
10" x 10' 4". Excellent
condition, c. 1920.
*Courtesy of Eliko
Antique & Decorative
Rugs.* Estimated value
$18,000.

Old Northwest Persian carpet. Vegetal dyes, wool pile, warp,
and weft, approx. 3' 5" x 11' 4". Slight wear, excellent
condition, c. 1910. *Courtesy of Christie's, Inc.* Estimated
value $9,000.

Old Caucasian Karabagh carpet. Synthetic and vegetal dyes,
wool pile, warp, and weft, approx. 3' 10" x 9' 6". Very slight
loss of pile in two corners, excellent condition, c. 1920.
Courtesy of Eliko Antique & Decorative Rugs. Estimated
value $6,500.

Old Caucasian Karabagh carpet. Probably synthetic dyes, wool pile, warp, and weft, approx. 5' x 12'. Very slight loss of pile on end, very good condition, c. 1920. *Courtesy of Kamali Oriental Rugs*. Estimated value $13,000.

Old Caucasian Kazak carpet. Vegetal dyes, wool pile, warp, and weft, approx. 5' 3" x 12' 7". Excellent condition, c. 1920. *Courtesy of Kamali Oriental Rugs*. Estimated value $14,000.

Old Caucasian Shirvan carpet. Vegetal dyes, wool pile, warp, and weft, approx. 4' 5" x 13' 9". Partially oxidized black wool, light wear, moderate wear on end border, good condition, c. 1900. *Courtesy of Christie's, Inc*. Estimated value $25,000.

Old Persian Senneh carpet. Vegetal dyes, wool pile, cotton warp and weft, approx. 8' x 11'. Excellent condition, c. 1930. *Courtesy of Kamali Oriental Rugs.* Estimated value $15,000.

Old Persian Bibikabad carpet. Vegetal dyes, wool pile, cotton warp and weft, approx. 9' 3" x 12' 1". Excellent condition, c. 1950. *Courtesy of Kamali Oriental Rugs.* Estimated value $9,000.

Above: Old Persian Senneh carpet. Vegetal dyes, wool pile, cotton warp and weft, approx. 8' 7" x 8' 10". Low in spots, very good condition, c. 1910. *Courtesy of Kamali Oriental Rugs.* Estimated value $15,000.

111

Old Persian Bakshaiash carpet. Vegetal dyes, wool pile, warp, and weft, approx. 7' 3" x 9' 8". Slight loss of pile on ends, heavy wear, repairs, fair condition, c. 1900. *Courtesy of Christie's, Inc.* Estimated value $17,000.

Old Persian Malayer carpet. Vegetal dyes, wool pile, cotton warp and weft, approx. 11' 6" x 12'. Moderate, even wear, good condition, c. 1910. *Courtesy of Kamali Oriental Rugs.* Estimated value $20,000.

Old Persian Heriz carpet. Vegetal dyes, wool pile, cotton warp and weft, approx. 5' 5" x 14' 1". Very slight loss of pile on end, low in spots, very good condition, c. 1920. *Courtesy of Kamali Oriental Rugs.* Estimated value $12,000.

Old Persian Heriz carpet. Vegetal dyes, wool pile, cotton warp and weft, approx. 7' 7" x 10' 1". Slight loss of pile on ends, very good condition, c. 1910. *Courtesy of Kamali Oriental Rugs.* Estimated value $12,000.

Old Persian Heriz carpet. Vegetal dyes, wool pile, cotton warp and weft, approx. 8' x 11'. Slight wear, very good condition, c. 1930. *Courtesy of Kamali Oriental Rugs.* Estimated value $12,000.

Old Persian Heriz carpet. Vegetal dyes, wool pile, cotton warp and weft, approx. 8' 2" x 11'. Slight wear, very good condition, c. 1920. *Courtesy of Kamali Oriental Rugs.* Estimated value $10,000.

Old Persian Heriz carpet. Vegetal dyes, wool pile, cotton warp and weft, approx. 8' 1" x 11' 7". Very slight loss of pile on end, slight wear, very good condition, c. 1920. *Courtesy of Kamali Oriental Rugs*. Estimated value $12,000.

Old Persian Serape carpet. Vegetal dyes, wool pile, cotton warp and weft, approx. 8' 5" x 11' 5". Loss of pile on sides and ends, moderate, even wear, good condition, c. 1900. *Courtesy of Kamali Oriental Rugs*. Estimated value $30,000.

Old Persian Heriz carpet. Vegetal dyes, wool pile, cotton warp and weft, approx. 8' 10" x 11' 10". Moderate, even wear, good condition, c. 1910. *Courtesy of Kamali Oriental Rugs*. Estimated value $21,000.

Old Persian Heriz carpet. Vegetal dyes, wool pile, cotton warp and weft, approx. 8' 9" x 11' 8". Excellent condition, c. 1940. *Courtesy of Kamali Oriental Rugs.* Estimated value $8,000.

Old Persian Serape carpet. Vegetal dyes, wool pile, cotton warp and weft, approx. 8' 11" x 11' 6". Moderate, even wear, good condition, c. 1890. *Courtesy of Kamali Oriental Rugs.* Estimated value $40,000.

Old Persian Serape carpet. Vegetal dyes, wool pile, cotton warp and weft, approx. 9' x 12' 9". Loss of pile on ends, light, even wear, very good condition, c. 1900. *Courtesy of Eliko Antique & Decorative Rugs.* Estimated value $50,000.

Old Persian Bakshaiash carpet. Vegetal dyes, wool pile, warp, and weft, approx. 9' 1" x 12' 10". Loss of pile on ends, moderate, even wear, very small repairs, good condition, c. 1890. *Courtesy of Christie's, Inc.* Estimated value $22,000.

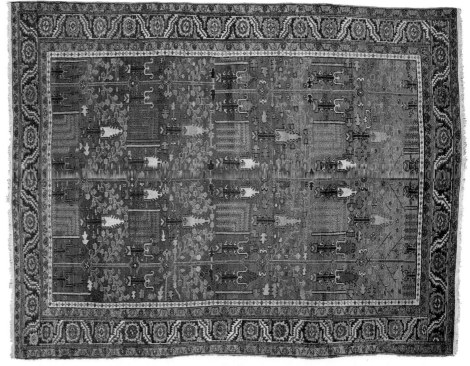

Old Persian Serape carpet. Vegetal dyes, wool pile, cotton warp and weft, approx. 9' 9" x 11' 9". Loss of pile on end, moderate wear, good condition, c. 1890. *Courtesy of Kamali Oriental Rugs.* Estimated value $24,000.

Old Persian Heriz carpet. Vegetal dyes, wool pile, cotton warp and weft, approx. 9' 9" x 12' 2". Moderate, even wear, very good condition, c. 1920. *Courtesy of Kamali Oriental Rugs.* Estimated value $15,000.

Old Persian Serape carpet. Vegetal dyes, wool pile, cotton warp and weft, approx. 9' 8" x 12' 4". Slight loss of pile on ends, slight wear, small repairs, very good condition, c. 1890. *Courtesy of Christie's, Inc.* Estimated value $35,000.

Old Persian Heriz carpet. Vegetal dyes, wool pile, cotton warp and weft, approx. 9' 2" x 12' 9". Loss of pile on ends, moderate, even wear, good condition, c. 1900. *Courtesy of Christie's, Inc.* Estimated value $30,000.

Old Persian Heriz carpet. Vegetal dyes, wool pile, cotton warp and weft, approx. 9' 6" x 12' 5". Loss of pile on ends, low in spots, very good condition, c. 1930. *Courtesy of Kamali Oriental Rugs.* Estimated value $14,000.

Above: Old Persian Serape carpet. Vegetal dyes, wool pile, cotton warp and weft, approx. 9' 2" x 12' 7". Very slight loss of pile on end, moderate wear, small repairs, good condition, c. 1900. *Courtesy of Kamali Oriental Rugs.* Estimated value $21,000.
Right: Old Persian Serape carpet. Vegetal dyes, wool pile, cotton warp and weft, approx. 9' 8" x 12' 11". Rewoven end borders, reselvedged, moderate, even wear, repairs, good condition, c. 1890. *Courtesy of Christie's, Inc.* Estimated value $20,000.

120

Opposite page:
Old Persian Serape carpet. Vegetal dyes, wool pile, cotton warp and weft, approx. 9' 11" x 12' 10". Slight loss of pile on end, excellent condition, c. 1900. *Courtesy of Abraham Moheban & Son.* Estimated value $55,000.

Above: Old Persian Serape carpet. Vegetal dyes, wool pile, cotton warp and weft, approx. 9' 6" x 13' 5". Moderate wear, small repairs, good condition, c. 1890. *Courtesy of Abraham Moheban & Son.* Estimated value $40,000.

Old Persian Heriz carpet. Vegetal dyes, wool pile, cotton warp and weft, approx. 8' 8" x 15'. Excellent condition, c. 1910. *Courtesy of Christie's, Inc.* Estimated value $30,000.

Old Persian Serape carpet. Vegetal dyes, wool pile, cotton warp and weft, approx. 9' 9" x 14'. Loss of pile on ends, slight wear, stains, very good condition, c. 1890. *Courtesy of Eliko Antique & Decorative Rugs.* Estimated value $85,000.

Old Persian Serape carpet. Vegetal dyes, wool pile, cotton warp and weft, approx. 11' 1" x 14' 10". Moderate wear, good condition, c. 1880. *Courtesy of Kamali Oriental Rugs.* Estimated value $60,000.

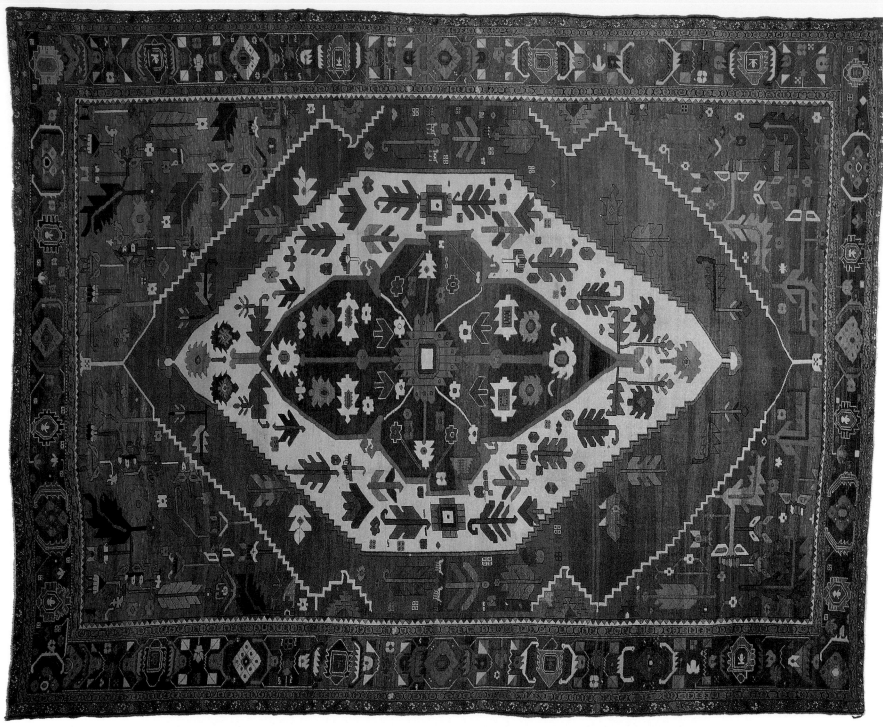

Old Persian Serape carpet. Vegetal dyes, wool pile, cotton warp and weft, approx. 12' x 14' 9". Slight wear, small repairs, very good condition, c. 1890. *Courtesy of Kamali Oriental Rugs*. Estimated value $60,000.

Old Persian Serape carpet. Vegetal dyes, wool pile, cotton warp and weft, approx. 11' 9" x 16' 6". Slight loss of pile on ends, low in spots, very good condition, c. 1890. *Courtesy of Eliko Antique & Decorative Rugs.* Estimated value $95,000.

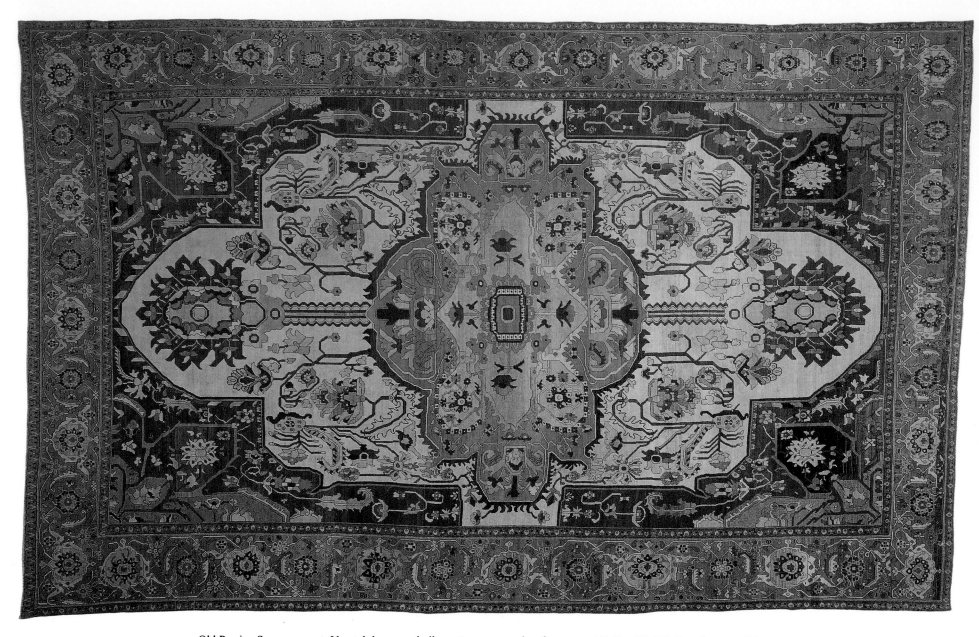

Old Persian Serape carpet. Vegetal dyes, wool pile, cotton warp and weft, approx. 11' 4" x 17' 10". Excellent condition, c. 1890. *Courtesy of Kamali Oriental Rugs.* Estimated value $120,000.

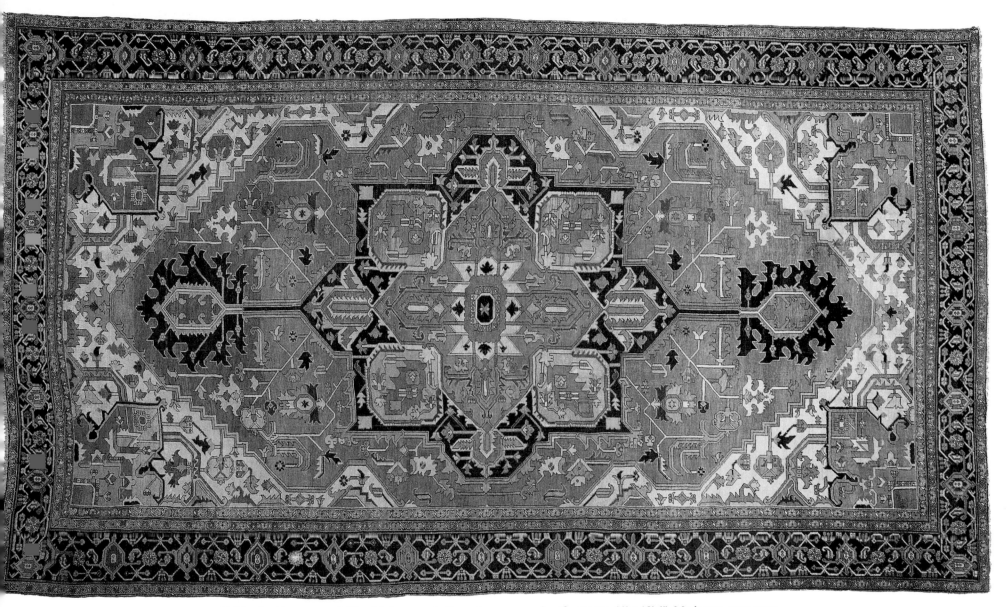

Old Persian Serape carpet. Vegetal dyes, wool pile, cotton warp and weft, approx. 11' x 18' 6". Moderate, even wear, small repairs and stains, good condition, c. 1900. *Courtesy of Kamali Oriental Rugs*. Estimated value $60,000.

Old Persian Serape carpet. Vegetal dyes, wool pile, cotton warp and weft, approx. 11' 6" x 18' 6". Very slight loss of pile on ends, slight wear, very good condition, c. 1900. *Courtesy of Kamali Oriental Rugs*. Estimated value $90,000.

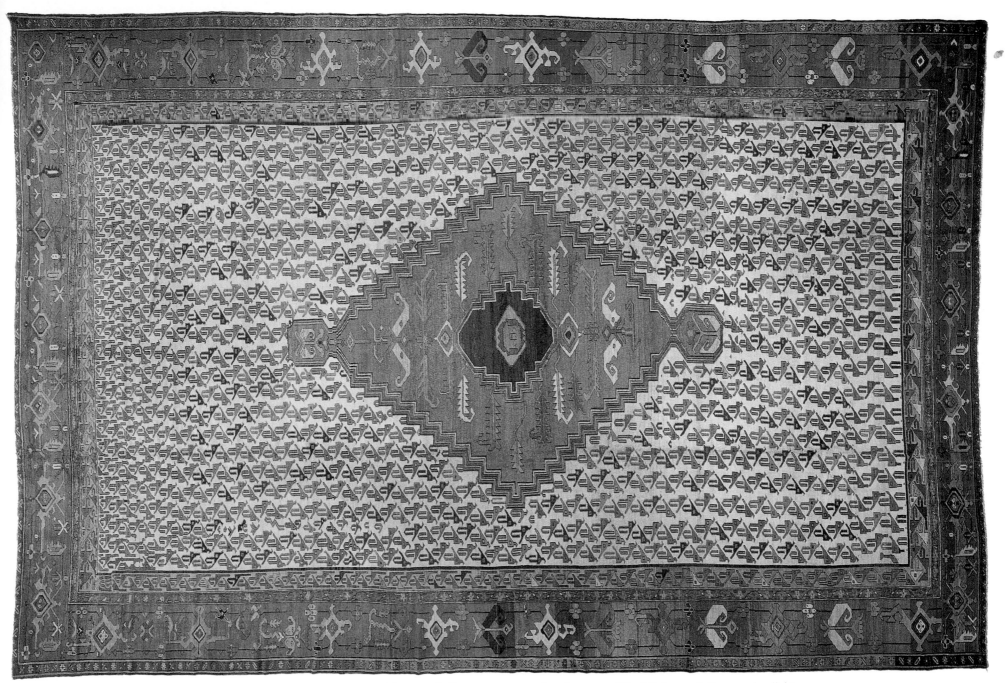

Old Persian Serape carpet. Vegetal dyes, wool pile, cotton warp and weft, approx. 12' x 18'. Loss of pile on ends, slight wear, very good condition, c. 1890. *Courtesy of Rahmanan Oriental Rugs.* Estimated value $60,000.

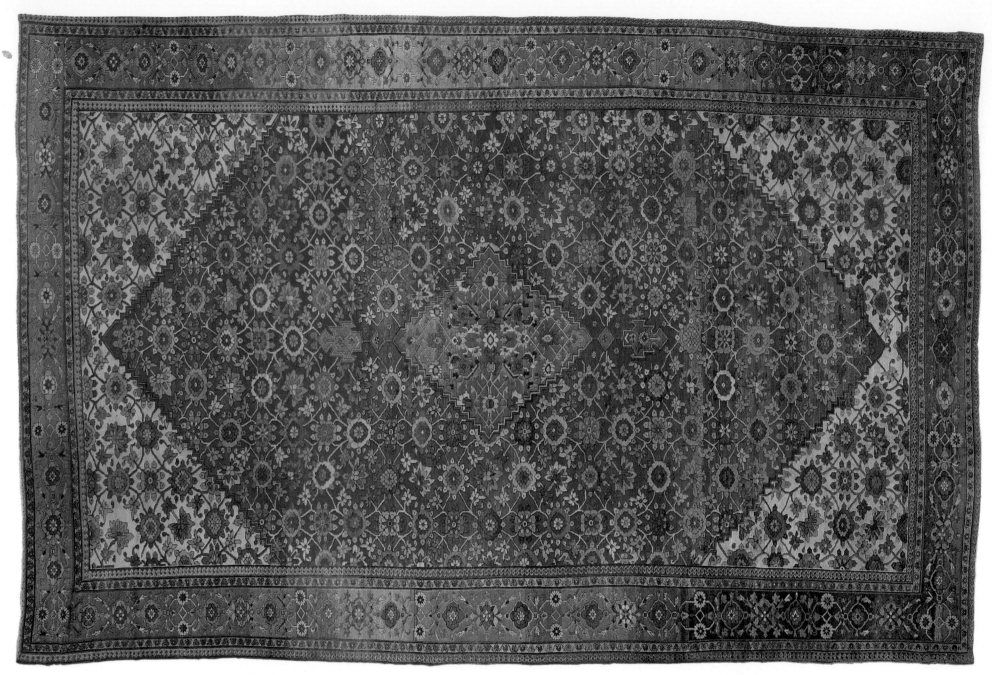

Old Persian Serape carpet. Vegetal dyes, wool pile, cotton warp and weft, approx. 13' 5" x 19' 9". Loss of one end guard border, slight wear, very good condition, c. 1910. *Courtesy of Kamali Oriental Rugs*. Estimated value $60,000.

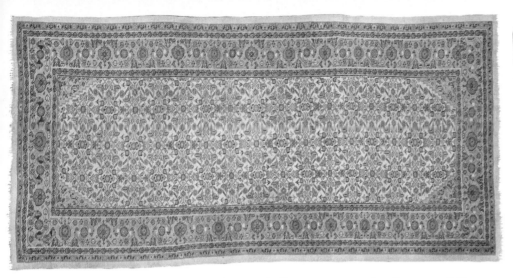

Old Persian Mahal carpet. Vegetal dyes, wool pile, cotton warp and weft, approx. 6' 6" x 12' 11". Moderate, even wear, good condition, c. 1920. *Courtesy of Kamali Oriental Rugs.* Estimated value $7,500.

Old Persian Mahal carpet. Vegetal dyes, wool pile, cotton warp and weft, approx. 8' 2" x 11' 6". Very good condition, c. 1940. *Courtesy of Kamali Oriental Rugs.* Estimated value $10,000.

Old Persian Mahal carpet. Vegetal dyes, wool pile, cotton warp and weft, approx. 8' 6" x 12'. Low in spots, very good condition, c. 1920. *Courtesy of Eliko Antique & Decorative Rugs.* Estimated value $20,000.

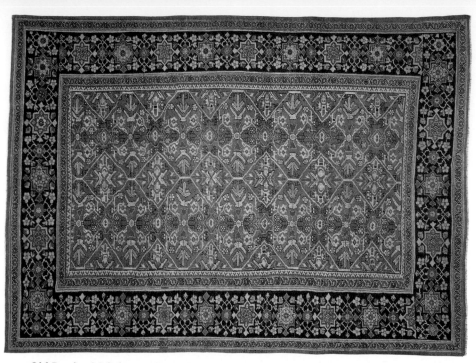

Old Persian Mahal carpet. Vegetal dyes, wool pile, cotton warp and weft, approx. 8' 9" x 11' 9". Moderate, even wear, good condition, c. 1910. *Courtesy of Kamali Oriental Rugs.* Estimated value $12,000.

Above: Old Persian Mahal carpet. Vegetal dyes, wool pile, cotton warp and weft, approx. 9' x 12'. Moderate, even wear, good condition, c. 1920. *Courtesy of Kamali Oriental Rugs.* Estimated value $15,000.

Left: Old Persian Mahal carpet. Vegetal dyes, wool pile, cotton warp and weft, approx. 8' 10" x 11' 7". Heavy wear, fair condition, c. 1910. *Courtesy of Kamali Oriental Rugs.* Estimated value $10,000.

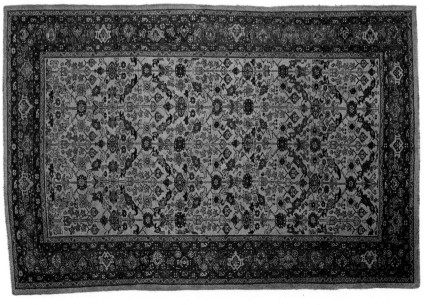

Above: Old Persian Mahal carpet. Vegetal dyes, wool pile, cotton warp and weft, approx. 9' 6" x 12' 2". Moderate, even wear, small repairs, good condition, c. 1900. *Courtesy of Christie's, Inc.* Estimated value $25,000.

Below: Old Persian Mahal carpet. Vegetal dyes, wool pile, cotton warp and weft, approx. 9' x 13'. Slight wear, very good condition, c. 1920. *Courtesy of Kamali Oriental Rugs.* Estimated value $14,000.

Old Persian Mahal carpet. Vegetal dyes, wool pile, cotton warp and weft, approx. 8' 10" x 12' 10". Slight wear, very good condition, c. 1910. *Courtesy of Kamali Oriental Rugs.* Estimated value $28,000.

Old Persian Mahal carpet. Vegetal dyes, wool pile, cotton warp and weft, approx. 10' 10" x 13' 7". Excellent condition, c. 1920. *Courtesy of Eliko Antique & Decorative Rugs.* Estimated value $45,000.

Old Persian Mahal carpet. Vegetal dyes, wool pile, cotton warp and weft, approx. 10' 10" x 13' 5". Excellent condition, c. 1920. *Courtesy of Eliko Antique & Decorative Rugs.* Estimated value $40,000.

Above: Old Persian Mahal carpet. Vegetal dyes, wool pile, cotton warp and weft, approx. 12' x 16'. Moderate, even wear, small repairs, good condition, c. 1920. *Courtesy of Eliko Antique & Decorative Rugs.* Estimated value $40,000.

Right: Old Persian Mahal carpet. Vegetal dyes, wool pile, cotton warp and weft, approx. 12' 2" x 19' 1". Low in spots, very good condition, c. 1930. *Courtesy of Kamali Oriental Rugs.* Estimated value $30,000.

Old Persian Sultanabad carpet. Vegetal dyes, wool pile, cotton warp and weft, approx. 11' 9" x 17' 1". Slight loss of pile on end, moderate wear, small, old repairs, good condition, c. 1900. *Courtesy of Eliko Antique & Decorative Rugs.* Estimated value $50,000.

Old Persian Sultanabad carpet. Vegetal dyes, wool pile, cotton warp and weft, approx. 14' 2" x 20' 2". Very slight loss of pile on end, excellent condition, c. 1910. *Courtesy of Eliko Antique & Decorative Rugs.* Estimated value $110,000.

Old Persian Bidjar carpet. Vegetal dyes, wool pile, warp, and weft, approx. 2' 6" x 10' 4". Loss of pile on ends, very good condition, c. 1920. *Courtesy of Eliko Antique & Decorative Rugs.* Estimated value $6,000.

Old Persian Bidjar carpet. Probably synthetic dyes, wool pile, warp, and weft, approx. 5' 7" x 12' 3". Very slight loss of pile on end, low in spots, very good condition, c. 1920. *Courtesy of Eliko Antique & Decorative Rugs.* Estimated value $14,000.

Old Persian Bidjar carpet. Vegetal dyes, wool pile, cotton warp and weft, approx. 5' 8" x 7' 7". Slight wear, very good condition, c. 1910. *Courtesy of Kamali Oriental Rugs.* Estimated value $12,000.

Old Persian Bidjar carpet. Vegetal dyes, wool pile, cotton warp and weft, approx. 7' 6" x 11' 7". Slight wear, very good condition, c. 1910. *Courtesy of Kamali Oriental Rugs*. Estimated value $20,000.

Old Persian Bidjar carpet. Vegetal dyes, wool pile, cotton warp and weft, approx. 7' 10" x 11' 9". Color run in end guard border, low in spots, good condition, c. 1920. *Courtesy of Kamali Oriental Rugs*. Estimated value $12,000.

Old Persian Bidjar carpet. Probably synthetic dyes, wool pile, warp, and weft, approx. 8' 3" x 11'. Slight wear, very good condition, c. 1920. *Courtesy of Eliko Antique & Decorative Rugs*. Estimated value $25,000.

Old Persian Bidjar carpet. Vegetal dyes, wool pile, cotton warp and weft, approx. 10' 6" x 13' 5". Excellent condition, c. 1910. *Courtesy of Kamali Oriental Rugs.* Estimated value $40,000.

Old Persian Bidjar carpet. Herati design. Vegetal dyes, wool pile, cotton warp and weft, approx. 11' 8" x 14' 5". Slight loss of pile on end, very good condition, c. 1910. *Courtesy of Kamali Oriental Rugs.* Estimated value $30,000.

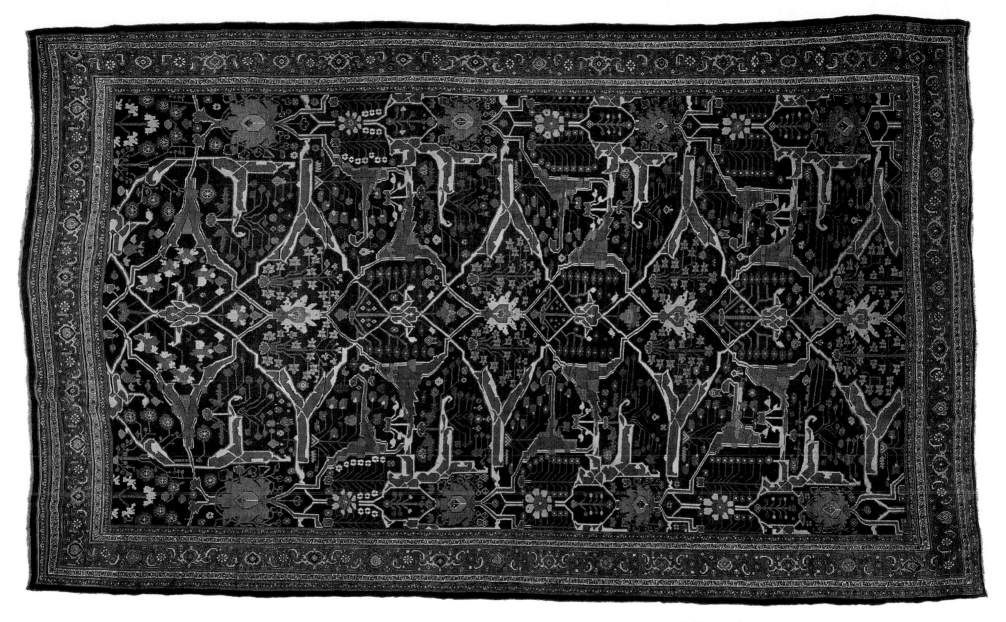

Old Persian Bidjar carpet. Vegetal dyes, wool pile, warp, and weft, approx. 11' x 17'. Slight loss of pile on end, moderate, even wear, good condition, c. 1890. *Courtesy of Rahmanan Oriental Rugs.* Estimated value $75,000.

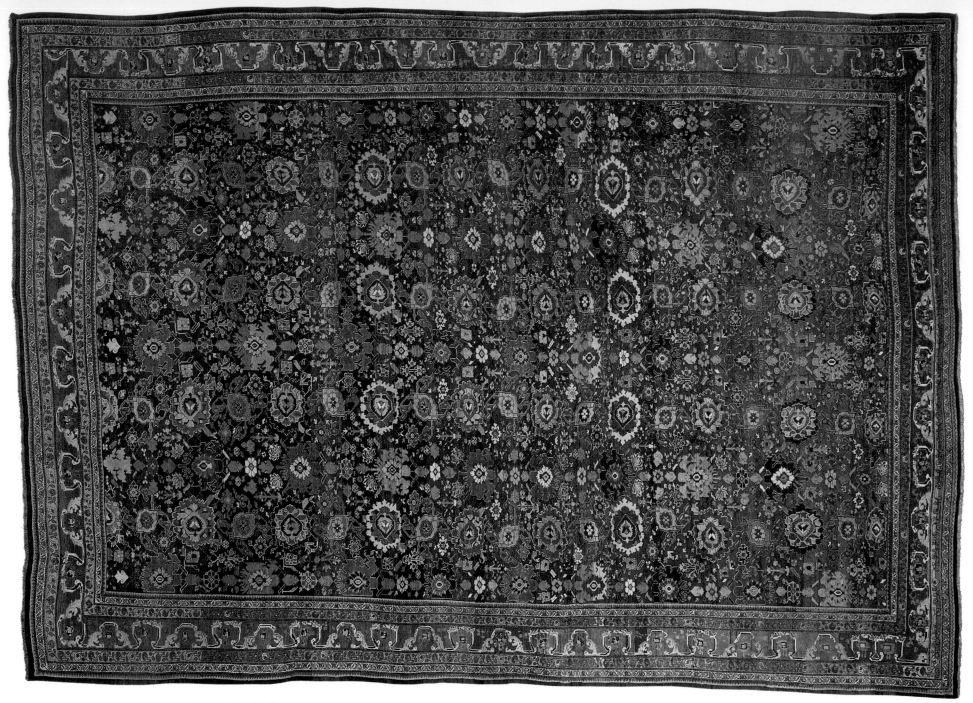

Old Persian Bidjar carpet. Vegetal dyes, wool pile, warp, and weft, approx. 13' 4" x 18' 6". Evenly low, very good condition, c. 1900. *Courtesy of Kamali Oriental Rugs.* Estimated value $75,000.

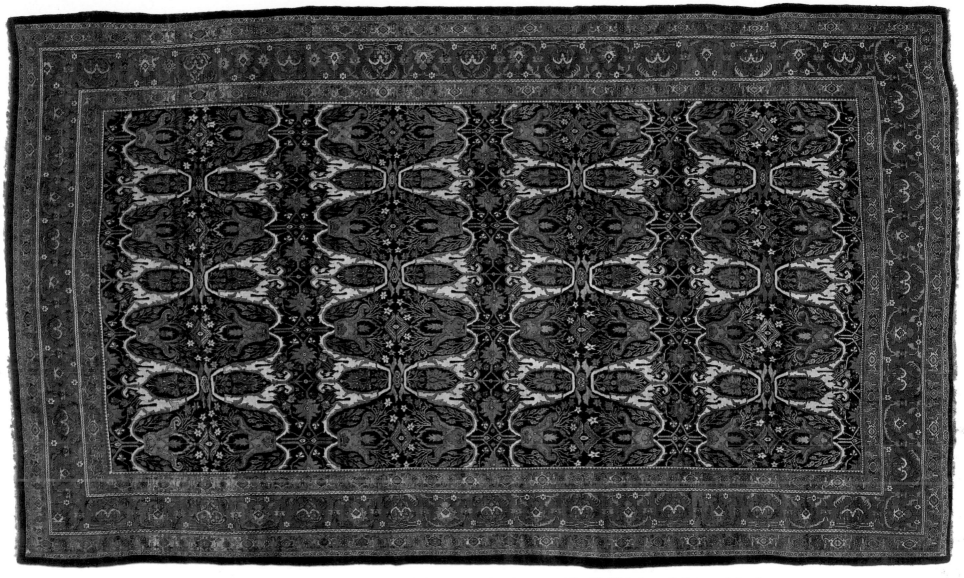

Old Persian Bidjar carpet. Vegetal dyes, wool pile, warp, and weft, approx. 15' x 25'. Slight loss of pile on end, low in spots, very good condition, c. 1920. *Courtesy of Rahmanan Oriental Rugs.* Estimated value $75,000.

Old Persian Ferahan Sarouk carpet. Vegetal dyes, wool pile, cotton warp and weft, approx. 6' 10" x 13' 2". Loss of pile on ends, slight wear, good condition, c. 1910. *Courtesy of Kamali Oriental Rugs.* Estimated value $9,000.

Old Persian Ferahan Sarouk carpet. Vegetal dyes, wool pile, cotton warp and weft, approx. 8' 5" x 11' 9". Loss of pile on end, moderate, even wear, good condition, c. 1890. *Courtesy of Kamali Oriental Rugs.* Estimated value $15,000.

Old Persian Ferahan Sarouk carpet. Vegetal dyes, wool pile, cotton warp and weft, approx. 7' x 9' 9". Slight wear, very good condition, c. 1910. *Courtesy of Kamali Oriental Rugs.* Estimated value $28,000.

Old Persian Ferahan Sarouk carpet. Vegetal dyes, wool pile, cotton warp and weft, approx. 9' x 11'. Excellent condition, c. 1910. *Courtesy of Kamali Oriental Rugs.* Estimated value $38,000.

Old Persian Ferahan Sarouk carpet. Vegetal dyes, wool pile, cotton warp and weft, approx. 9' x 12'. Loss of pile on ends, moderate, even wear, good condition, c. 1890. *Courtesy of N. Ben Chafieian Oriental Rugs.* Estimated value $48,000.

Old Persian Sarouk carpet. Vegetal dyes, wool pile, cotton warp and weft, approx. 8' 10" x 11' 9". Very good condition, c. 1930. *Courtesy of Kamali Oriental Rugs.* Estimated value $10,000.

Above: Old Persian Mahajeran Sarouk carpet. Vegetal dyes, wool pile, cotton warp and weft, approx. 8' 10" x 12' 5". Excellent condition, c. 1910. *Courtesy of Eliko Antique & Decorative Rugs.* Estimated value $27,000.
Left: Old Persian Kazvin carpet. Vegetal dyes, wool pile, cotton warp and weft, approx. 9' x 12'. Excellent condition, c. 1920. *Courtesy of Kamali Oriental Rugs.* Estimated value $16,000.

Old Persian Sarouk carpet. Vegetal dyes, wool pile, cotton warp and weft, approx. 9' 2" x 12' 2". Low in spots, very good condition, c. 1920. *Courtesy of Kamali Oriental Rugs.* Estimated value $15,000.

Old Persian Sarouk carpet. Vegetal dyes, wool pile, cotton warp and weft, approx. 8' x 15'. Excellent condition, c. 1920. *Courtesy of Kamali Oriental Rugs.* Estimated value $15,000.

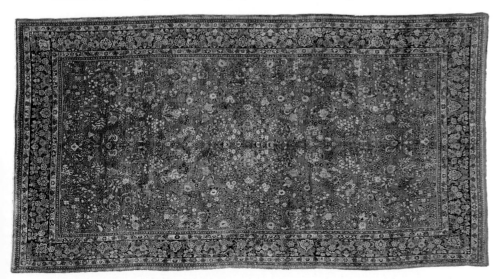

Old Persian Sarouk carpet. Vegetal dyes, wool pile, cotton warp and weft, approx. 10' 6" x 11' 6". Excellent condition, c. 1920. *Courtesy of Kamali Oriental Rugs.* Estimated value $18,000.

Old Persian Mahajeran Sarouk carpet. Vegetal dyes, wool pile, cotton warp and weft, approx. 10' 2" x 13' 5". Slight wear, good condition, c. 1910. *Courtesy of Kamali Oriental Rugs*. Estimated value $20,000.

Old Persian Sarouk carpet. Vegetal dyes, wool pile, cotton warp and weft, approx. 10' x 14'. Excellent condition, c. 1920. *Courtesy of Kamali Oriental Rugs*. Estimated value $36,000.

Old Persian Mahajeran Sarouk carpet. Vegetal dyes, wool pile, cotton warp and weft, approx. 10' 5" x 13' 8". Low in spots, very good condition, c. 1910. *Courtesy of Kamali Oriental Rugs*. Estimated value $16,000.

Above: Old Persian Sarouk carpet. Vegetal dyes, wool pile, cotton warp and weft, approx. 12' 2" x 13' 6". Excellent condition, c. 1930. *Courtesy of Kamali Oriental Rugs.* Estimated value $30,000.

Top right: Old Persian Lillihan carpet. Vegetal dyes, wool pile, cotton warp and weft, approx. 8' 10" x 11' 9". Slight design imbalance in main field, slight wear, good condition, c. 1930. *Courtesy of Kamali Oriental Rugs.* Estimated value $12,000.

Bottom right: Old Persian Lillihan carpet. Vegetal dyes, wool pile, cotton warp and weft, approx. 9' 6" x 11' 9". Excellent condition, c. 1930. *Courtesy of Kamali Oriental Rugs.* Estimated value $12,000.

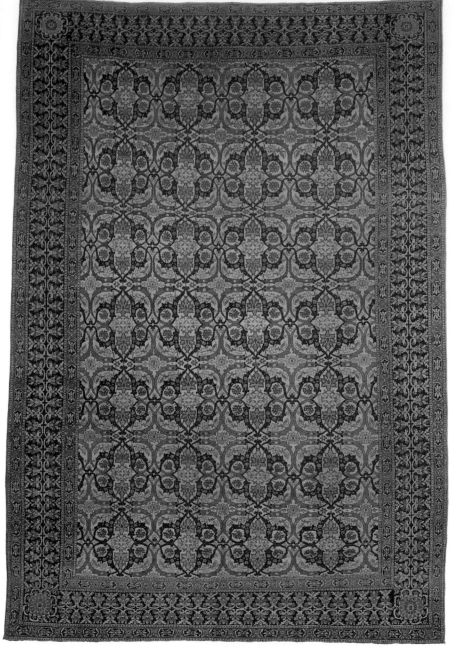

Above: Old Persian Tabriz carpet. Probably synthetic dyes, wool pile, cotton warp and weft, approx. 7' 4" x 10' 9". Slight loss of pile on end, slight wear, very good condition, c. 1920. *Courtesy of Eliko Antique & Decorative Rugs.* Estimated value $20,000.

Left: Old Persian Tabriz carpet. Vegetal dyes, wool pile, cotton warp and weft, approx. 6' x 10'. Evenly low, very good condition, c. 1920. *Courtesy of Kamali Oriental Rugs.* Estimated value $24,000.

Old Persian Tabriz carpet. Vegetal dyes, wool pile, cotton warp and weft, approx. 9' 6" x 12'. Slight wear, very good condition, c. 1910. *Courtesy of Eliko Antique & Decorative Rugs.* Estimated value $40,000.

Old Persian Hadji Jahlili Tabriz carpet. Vegetal dyes, wool pile, cotton warp and weft, approx. 9' x 12' 5". Very slight loss of pile on end, very good condition, c. 1890. *Courtesy of Eliko Antique & Decorative Rugs.* Estimated value $36,000.

Old Persian Tabriz carpet. Synthetic dyes, wool pile, cotton warp and weft, approx. 9' 5" x 12' 5". Light, even wear, good condition, c. 1910. *Courtesy of Eliko Antique & Decorative Rugs.* Estimated value $28,000.

Opposite page:
Old Persian Hadji Jahlili Tabriz carpet. Vegetal dyes, wool pile, cotton warp and weft, approx. 11' 2" x 14' 7". Excellent condition, c. 1900. *Courtesy of Eliko Antique & Decorative Rugs.* Estimated value $150,000.

Old Persian Tabriz carpet. Vegetal dyes, wool pile, cotton warp and weft, approx. 10' 3" x 14' 3". Slight wear, small stains, very good condition, c. 1920. *Courtesy of Kamali Oriental Rugs.* Estimated value $33,000.

Old Persian Tabriz carpet. Vegetal dyes, wool pile, cotton warp and weft, approx. 11' 1" x 15' 1". Low in spots, very good condition, c. 1930. *Courtesy of Kamali Oriental Rugs.* Estimated value $24,000.

Old Persian Tabriz carpet. Vegetal dyes, wool pile, cotton warp and weft, approx. 10' 4" x 18'. Excellent condition, c. 1910. *Courtesy of Hasid Oriental Rugs, Inc.* Estimated value $80,000.

Right: Old Persian Kerman carpet. Vegetal dyes, wool pile, cotton warp and weft, approx. 4' x 11'. Slight wear, very good condition, c. 1920. *Courtesy of Kamali Oriental Rugs.* Estimated value $14,000.

Left: Old Persian Hadji Jahlili Tabriz carpet. Mir-i boteh design. Vegetal dyes, wool pile, cotton warp and weft, approx. 11' 5" x 18'. Small stain, excellent condition, c. 1910. *Courtesy of Abraham Moheban & Son.* Estimated value $90,000.

155

Old Persian Lavar Kerman carpet. Vegetal dyes, wool pile, cotton warp and weft, approx. 5' 6" x 8' 6". Slight wear, very good condition, c. 1890. *Courtesy of Kamali Oriental Rugs.* Estimated value $16,000.

Old Persian Lavar Kerman carpet. Vegetal dyes, wool pile, cotton warp and weft, approx. 5' 10" x 9' 6". Heavy wear, fair condition, c. 1890. *Courtesy of Kamali Oriental Rugs.* Estimated value $16,000.

Old Persian Lavar Kerman carpet. Vegetal dyes, wool pile, cotton warp and weft, approx. 5' 10" x 9' 3". Slight wear, very good condition, c. 1910. *Courtesy of Eliko Antique & Decorative Rugs.* Estimated value $20,000.

Old Persian Kerman carpet. Vegetal dyes, wool pile, cotton warp and weft, approx. 8' 7" x 11' 5". Very good condition, c. 1920. *Courtesy of Kamali Oriental Rugs.* Estimated value $15,000.

Above: Old Persian Kerman carpet. Vegetal dyes, wool pile, cotton warp and weft, approx. 8' 8" x 11' 11". Excellent condition, c. 1920. *Courtesy of Kamali Oriental Rugs.* Estimated value $20,000.
Left: Old Persian Kerman carpet. Vegetal dyes, wool pile, cotton warp and weft, approx. 10' 5" x 11' 9". Very good condition, c. 1930. *Courtesy of Kamali Oriental Rugs.* Estimated value $12,000.

Old Persian Kerman carpet. Vegetal dyes, wool pile, cotton warp and weft, approx. 9' 8" x 16' 1". Slight wear, good condition, c. 1920. *Courtesy of Kamali Oriental Rugs*. Estimated value $18,000.

Old Persian Kerman carpet. Vegetal dyes, wool pile, cotton warp and weft, approx. 9' 8" x 13' 6". Slight wear, good condition, c. 1930. *Courtesy of Kamali Oriental Rugs*. Estimated value $12,000.

Old Persian Kerman carpet. Vegetal dyes, wool pile, cotton warp and weft, approx. 10' 8" x 14' 7". Low in spots, good condition, c. 1920. *Courtesy of Kamali Oriental Rugs*. Estimated value $17,500.

Right: Old Persian Kerman carpet. Vegetal dyes, wool pile, cotton warp and weft, approx. 12' 7" x 24' 5". Very good condition, c. 1920. *Courtesy of Kamali Oriental Rugs.* Estimated value $55,000.

Left: Old Persian Lavar Kerman carpet. Vegetal dyes, wool pile, cotton warp and weft, approx. 9' 6" x 17' 2". Excellent condition, c. 1890. *Courtesy of Kamali Oriental Rugs.* Estimated value $45,000.

Old Persian Kashan carpet. Vegetal dyes, wool pile, cotton warp and weft, approx. 8' 9" x 11' 6". Excellent condition, c. 1920. *Courtesy of Kamali Oriental Rugs.* Estimated value $18,000.

Old Persian Isfahan carpet. Vegetal dyes, wool pile, silk warp and weft, approx. 6' 10" x 10' 7". Excellent condition, c. 1950. *Courtesy of Kamali Oriental Rugs.* Estimated value $23,000.

160

Old Persian Teheran carpet. Zele Sultan design. Vegetal dyes, wool pile, cotton warp and weft, approx. 10' 6" x 13' 8". Excellent condition, c. 1930. *Courtesy of Kamali Oriental Rugs*. Estimated value $36,000.

Old Indian Amritsar carpet. Vegetal dyes, wool pile, cotton warp and weft, approx. 7' x 10'. Slight wear, very good condition, c. 1910. *Courtesy of Abraham Moheban & Son*. Estimated value $22,000.

Old Indian Amritsar carpet. Vegetal dyes, wool pile, cotton warp and weft, approx. 10' x 12'. Moderate, even wear, good condition, c. 1910. *Courtesy of Rahmanan Oriental Rugs.* Estimated value $35,000.

Old Indian Amritsar carpet. Vegetal dyes, wool pile, cotton warp and weft, approx. 9' 11" x 13' 4". Excellent condition, c. 1900. *Courtesy of Abraham Moheban & Son.* Estimated value $45,000.

Right: Old Indian carpet. Vegetal dyes, wool pile, cotton warp and weft, approx. 10' x 15'. Excellent condition, c. 1930. *Courtesy of Kamali Oriental Rugs.* Estimated value $23,000.

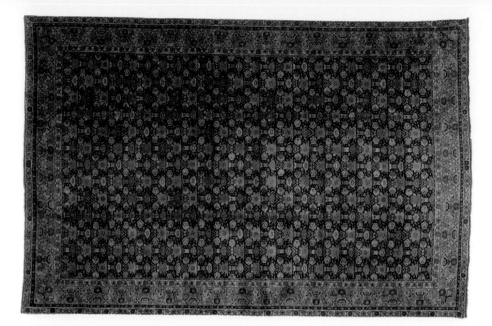

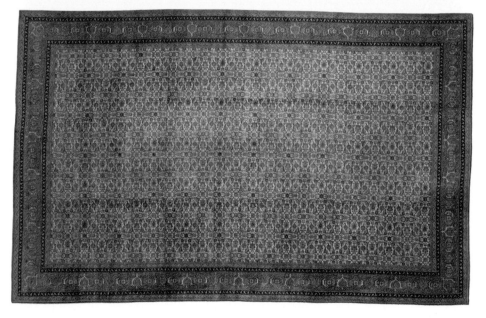

Old Indian Agra carpet. Vegetal dyes, wool pile, cotton warp and weft, approx. 10' 1" x 13' 1". Very slight loss of pile on end, partial oxidization of garnet wool, slight moth damage on edge, slight wear, good condition, c. 1910. *Courtesy of Christie's, Inc.* Estimated value $30,000.

Above: Old Indian carpet. Herati design. Vegetal dyes, wool pile, cotton warp and weft, approx. 10' x 16'. Excellent condition, c. 1920. *Courtesy of Kamali Oriental Rugs.* Estimated value $25,000.

Opposite page, *left:* Old Indian carpet. Millefleurs prayer design. Vegetal dyes, wool pile, cotton warp and weft, approx. 10' 6" x 16'. Slight wear, good condition, c. 1920. *Courtesy of Kamali Oriental Rugs.* Estimated value $30,000.

Right: Old Indian carpet. Vegetal dyes, wool pile, cotton warp and weft, approx. 12' x 19' 8". Very good condition, c. 1920. *Courtesy of Kamali Oriental Rugs.* Estimated value $45,000.

Old Turkish Oushak carpet. Vegetal dyes, wool pile, warp, and weft, approx. 7' 10" x 10' 7". Very good condition, c. 1920. *Courtesy of Kamali Oriental Rugs.* Estimated value $20,000.

Old Turkish Sivas carpet. Vegetal dyes, wool pile, cotton warp and weft, approx. 9' x 12'. Slight loss of pile in corner, excellent condition, c. 1910. *Courtesy of Rahmanan Oriental Rugs.* Estimated value $65,000.

Old Turkish Oushak carpet. Vegetal dyes, wool pile, warp, and weft, approx. 8' x 11'. Slight wear, very good condition, c. 1920. *Courtesy of Kamali Oriental Rugs.* Estimated value $18,000.

Above: Old Turkish Oushak carpet. Vegetal dyes, wool pile, warp, and weft, approx. 9' 3" x 12' 7". Excellent condition, c. 1910. *Courtesy of Abraham Moheban & Son.* Estimated value $24,000.
Left: Old Turkish Oushak carpet. Vegetal dyes, wool pile, warp, and weft, approx. 8' 7" x 11' 6". Moderate wear, very good condition, c. 1920. *Courtesy of Kamali Oriental Rugs.* Estimated value $16,000.

Old Turkish Oushak carpet. Vegetal dyes, wool pile, warp, and weft, approx. 9' 9" x 13'. Small stains, very good condition, c. 1910. *Courtesy of Kamali Oriental Rugs.* Estimated value $16,000.

Old Turkish Oushak carpet. Vegetal dyes, wool pile, warp, and weft, approx. 10' x 12'. Very light loss of pile on ends, slight sunfading, moderate wear, good condition, c. 1920. *Courtesy of Kamali Oriental Rugs.* Estimated value $16,000.

Old Turkish Oushak carpet. Vegetal dyes, wool pile, cotton warp and weft, approx. 10' x 13' 5". Very good condition, c. 1940. *Courtesy of Kamali Oriental Rugs.* Estimated value $15,000.

Old Turkish Oushak carpet. Vegetal dyes, wool pile, cotton warp and weft, approx. 11' 10" x 12' 2". Excellent condition, c. 1910. *Courtesy of Eliko Antique & Decorative Rugs.* Estimated value $32,000.

Old Turkish Oushak Carpet. Vegetal dyes, wool pile, warp, and weft, approx. 12' 6" x 16' 6". Low in spots, very good condition, c. 1920. *Courtesy of Kamali Oriental Rugs.* Estimated value $45,000.

169

Old Betzalel or Jerusalem carpet. Vegetal dyes, wool pile, cotton warp and weft, approx. 5' 6" x 7' 7". Low in spots, very good condition, c. 1930. *Courtesy of Eliko Antique & Decorative Rugs.* Estimated value $9,000.

Old Spanish carpet. Vegetal dyes, wool pile, cotton warp and weft, approx. 9' 7" x 9' 7". Slight loss of pile on ends, moderate, even wear, small stain, good condition, c. 1910. *Courtesy of Eliko Antique & Decorative Rugs.* Estimated value $20,000.

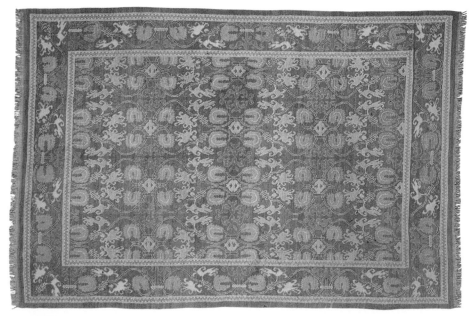

Old Spanish carpet. Probably chrome dyes, wool pile, cotton warp and weft, approx. 6' 7" x 9' 7". Excellent condition, c. 1950. *Courtesy of Kamali Oriental Rugs.* Estimated value $6,000.

Above: Old European carpet. Probably synthetic dyes, wool pile, cotton warp and weft, approx. 11' 9" x 17' 6". Excellent condition, c. 1940. *Courtesy of Kamali Oriental Rugs.* Estimated value $18,000.

Left: Old French Savonnerie carpet. Probably synthetic dyes, wool pile, cotton warp and weft, approx. 11' 3" x 16' 10". Excellent condition, c. 1920. *Courtesy of Abraham Moheban & Son.* Estimated value $45,000.

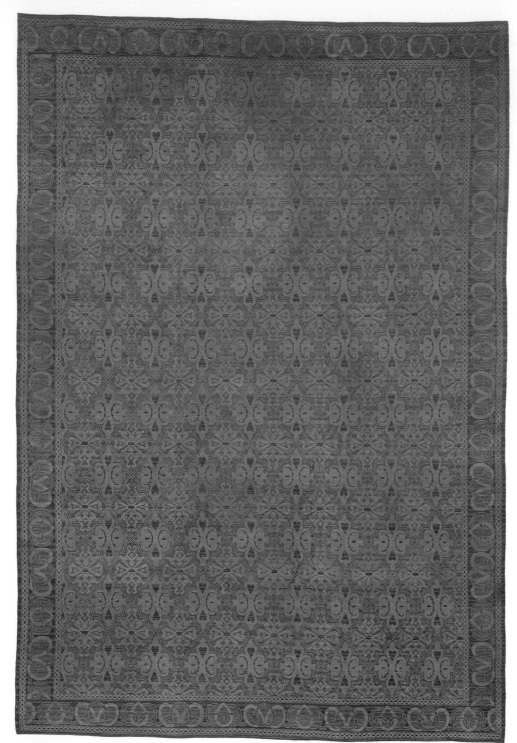

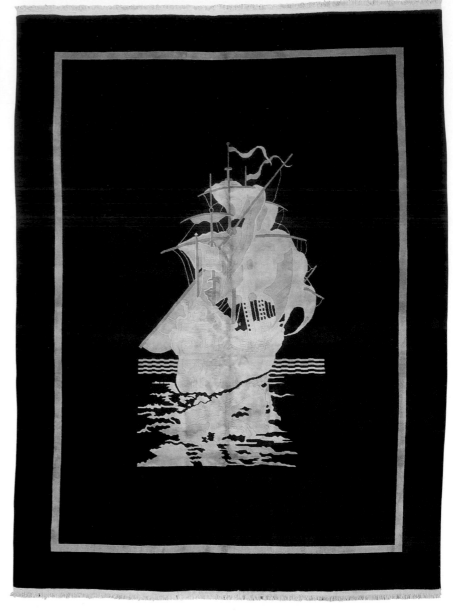

Old Nichols Chinese carpet. Synthetic dyes, wool pile, cotton warp and weft, approx. 8' 9" x 11' 7". Excellent condition, c. 1930. *Courtesy of Kamali Oriental Rugs.* Estimated value $12,000.

Old Spanish carpet. Synthetic and vegetal dyes, wool pile, jute warp and weft, approx. 12' x 18'. Excellent condition, c. 1920. *Courtesy of Rahmanan Oriental Rugs.* Estimated value $45,000.

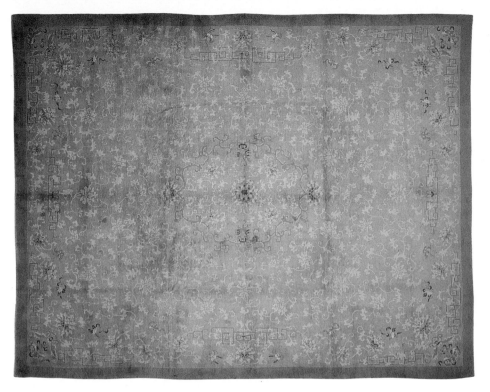

Old Chinese carpet. Vegetal dyes, wool pile, cotton warp and weft, approx. 8' 6" x 11' 6". Slight moth damage on edge, sunfaded area, good condition, c. 1930. *Courtesy of Kamali Oriental Rugs.* Estimated value $10,000.

Old Peking Chinese carpet. Vegetal dyes, wool pile, cotton warp and weft, approx. 9' x 11' 6". Low in spots, very good condition, c. 1910. *Courtesy of Kamali Oriental Rugs.* Estimated value $15,000.

Old Peking Chinese carpet. Vegetal dyes, wool pile, cotton warp and weft, approx. 8' 6" x 11' 6". Slight moth damage and small repairs on edge, very good condition, c. 1920. *Courtesy of Kamali Oriental Rugs.* Estimated value $20,000.

173

Old Peking Chinese carpet. Vegetal dyes, wool pile, cotton warp and weft, approx. 9' x 12'. Excellent condition, c. 1910. *Courtesy of Kamali Oriental Rugs.* Estimated value $25,000.

is silk, a dealer might pull off a small piece of pile or warp thread and burn it. If the smoke has a distinctive organic smell, the rug is probably silk. Kashan silks are excellent, but rarely crop up in the trade and are usually quite worn. Tabriz and Heriz silks, often in prayer designs reminiscent of mosque domed architecture, are highly prized if in very good condition, but are also scarce today. Metallic thread generally adds value to these pieces. A fine old Kashan, Tabriz, or Heriz silk in very good condition, 4 x 6 feet, generally retails for about $25,000 or more depending upon character, color, rarity, and fineness.

Antique, room-sized Persian silk Tabrizes and Herizes are arguably the most coveted antique carpets in the trade, with the possible exception of court and very rare, early rugs found in museums. They may sell for hundreds of thousands of dollars and arouse much interest when they appear in auctions.

New small-sized silks with fine weaves in Persian designs from China may be excellent investments if well bought and often belong on walls rather than floors. Silk has been an integral part of the culture of China for millenia, and Chinese silk carpets are the best, and least expensive, in the world. Birds and other animals should be realistically drawn and, if possible, not too rigidly ordered when found in these little gems. Many new rugs from China have the appearance and feel of silk but are made from other fibers.

Silk Rugs

Old silk carpets are highly regarded in the trade. Care must be taken to avoid overpaying for rugs that look like silk but are actually mercerized cotton such as certain Turkish Kayseri pieces. To determine if an antique carpet

Old Persian Kashan silk carpet. Vegetal dyes, silk pile, warp, and weft, approx. 4' 3" x 6' 9". Excellent condition, c. 1920. *Courtesy of Christie's, Inc.* Estimated value $20,000.

Old Persian Heriz silk carpet. Vegetal dyes, silk pile, warp, and weft, approx. 9' 4" x 12' 9". Excellent condition, c. 1890. *Courtesy of Christie's, Inc.* Estimated value $100,000.

176

Big is Beautiful

About twenty years ago the dealer interest in small old rugs—2 x 4 to 4 x 6 feet—diminished because these pieces became more expensive relative to room-sized carpets. Dealers became more desirous of large rugs because of their better value per square foot. On 57th Street in New York City, where spaces are relatively small and rents are high, retailers have very few small-sized weavings. Slightly worn, old, oversized, formal Persian carpets such as Kashans and Sarouks, 12 x 18 feet or larger, may still be good values. Very large new pieces are also generally desirable because they are rarer and more difficult to perfectly execute than smaller carpets.

Great care should be taken in purchasing small old rugs because they are sometimes either unimportant and not worth buying or important and over-priced. Wholesalers may be a source for good values in these weavings. Try to find examples with beautiful old vegetable dyes in which no individual hue stands out too strongly against other soft and muted colors. Although it is easier to examine a small weaving, it is usually safer to acquire a larger carpet because it will probably be a better buy.

Designing Tips

One should begin to design a room with the floor covering, if possible, particularly if one desires an expensive old carpet. It is not practical to look for an antique rug to blend with a swatch of fabric. In these days of increased scarcity, extensive restoration may be required for that unique old piece that blends with previously purchased fabrics. Non-descript, pale carpets are highly desirable in the decorator trade because the vast majority of designers begin with busy drapery and upholstery fabrics and then purchase carpet. If more decorators began with floor covering they would have a wider selection of rugs with deeply saturated colors for their clients.

Start with a beautiful carpet and then search for all the other appointments to complement it. The rug does not have to match the other elements exactly, and fine detailing is sometimes more important than precisely complementing colors. However, the style of the carpet should parallel the feeling of the neighboring textiles, including other rugs. Delicate upholstery and drapery design normally matches ornate, formal rugs and informal fabric patterns harmonize with casual, often geometric weavings. Semi-formal carpets are usually compatible with either formal or informal rugs and furnishings.

Intricate patterned fabric ordinarily blends with a less-detailed, more open-designed carpet. More complex upholstery designs generally coordinate with complicated rug patterns only if colors are very closely correlated. Although one should not put a coarse sisal mat next to French rococo furniture, one may place an inexpensive carpet adjacent to an expensive piece of furniture, if they complement one another stylistically.

The dining room rug must be large enough for the chairs to slide back and forth without catching the selvedges and ends. A minimum of two feet of carpet should surround the table, if possible. An overall rather than central medallion design is preferred for this room, and the rug should have an interesting and powerful border. The center field design is rather unimportant and may be simply a prosaic repeat pattern. Piled carpets are better than kilims, needlepoints, or Aubussons as the latter are generally too delicate for the movement of chairs.

Any sized rug may be used in any room in which it can fit, and there are no fixed rules for designing an area. A small piece may lie under a table in the corner of a large room, or an area may be filled with scatter rugs. Rug lovers will frequently put discrete or disjunctive weavings adjacent to one another.

The bedroom normally requires small to medium sized weavings around the bed, or one large overall designed carpet that covers most of the room. The area rugs may be related in either or both color and design. They should preferably be of high quality and special beauty because it is always nice to wake up to an exalting carpet or kilim.

A rug with a central medallion may be used in the living room but it is easier to decorate with an overall designed piece. The medallion is often difficult to center below a coffee table or parallel to a fireplace or mantlepiece. Ideally, the living room carpet should have a lovely main field and an alluring border.

If a section of the rug must be cut and removed to accomodate a fireplace, it should be retained for reattachment, if necessary, at a later date. If the piece is lost, the value of the carpet is significantly reduced. The edge of the rug that encircles the fireplace should be bound by hand to prevent unraveling.

The hallway may require a light-colored piece to brighten up a dark area. Long wide runners, if required, are hard to find, so a pair of matching, or closely related, pieces should be placed one after the other as a substitute.

A heavily trafficked foyer may require a strong, thick, and dark-colored carpet that will stay clean longer. Often a dense, intricate pattern will not show dirt as easily as an open field design.

Imperfections In Old Carpets

Discordant Abrash

Most old carpets have slight variations or subtle changes of tone within certain colors. This is caused by the fact that one dyelot may yield more or less intense color than the next, or because the dye changes after many skeins of wool are emersed in the dyebath. Abrash may also result from the use of different mordants, or elements that help the dye cling to the wool, and variations in the structure of each skein of yarn. Occasionally, abrashed areas wear more quickly because inferior wool, or corrosive dyes, have been used in the rug.

Abrash is generally a good feature as long as it is harmonious and gradual. Bad abrash is a blatant, distracting, or disturbing color change and is a serious flaw. If the abrash is only found on the top end or half of the carpet, an imperfection usually results.

If a completely new, excessively obtrusive color is woven across a large section of the rug, the flaw may also be present.

Striking abrash is quite common in some of the new geometric rugs from Turkey, Nepal, and India. More license may be given to creative imbalanced tonal variations within individual colors in these carpets. Abrash helps make most rugs unique and generally adds to collectibility.

Broken Lazy Lines

Certain carpets such as Herizes and Serapes may have diagonal lines or seams of various lengths, about twelve inches or longer, visible on the back of the rug. This phenomenon occurs when the weaver works in sections instead of weaving all the way across the width of the carpet. As each block is woven, the horizontal wefts that run over and under the vertical warps, and hold each row of knots in place, are returned to the edges from which they came, instead of continued across the length of the rug. A staggered line is formed at the points where the sections meet. "Lazy" lines are not imperfections in spite of many people's beliefs to the contrary; however, they slightly weaken the foundation of the areas in which they are found. On rare occasions, the carpet is stretched, the seams split apart, and must be sewn together again. Then the "lazy" lines become a significant flaw in the piece.

"Lazy" lines are common in kilims as individual colors are built up block by block. They are not imperfections but ways in which the weaver injects variety into different areas of solid color.

less desirable, unbalanced abrash

Abrash, or tonal variations within colors.

better, balanced abrash

Abrash, or tonal variations within colors.

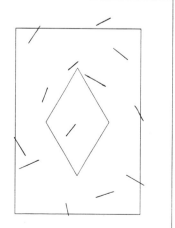

Lazy lines, or staggered wefts visible in kilims and backs of certain piled carpets.

Shape Irregularities

Rugs should be a fair approximation of a rectangle or square in shape. Some allowance may be tolerated but the carpet must not be disturbingly trapezoidal. The length of one edge should preferably not be more than about one to three inches greater than the other edge of the weaving. The width of one end must also not be more than approximately one to three inches greater than the other end of the piece. Usually, the smaller the rug, the less shape imbalance is acceptable. A misshapen carpet may be professionally stretched very slightly, but generally this is not advisable because there is always a risk of splitting the foundation. The piece may also eventually revert to its irregular form. Slight curves or small variations in length or width are fine, and often add to the quaintness of the piece. More noticeable curves and bumps may be serious flaws depending upon the degree of crookedness or irregularity. Greater curvature is permitted in tribal or village weavings than formal city carpets.

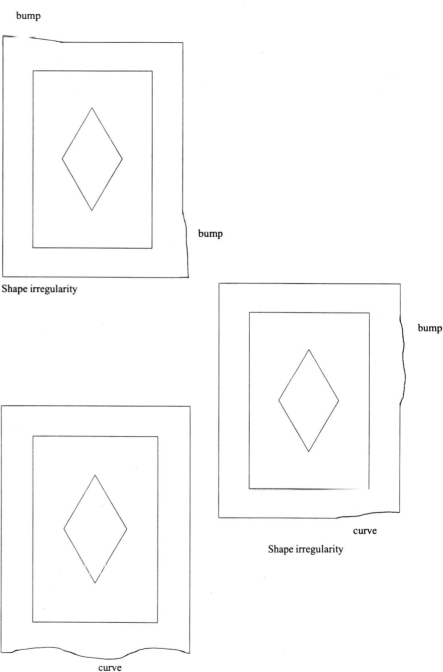

bump

bump

Shape irregularity

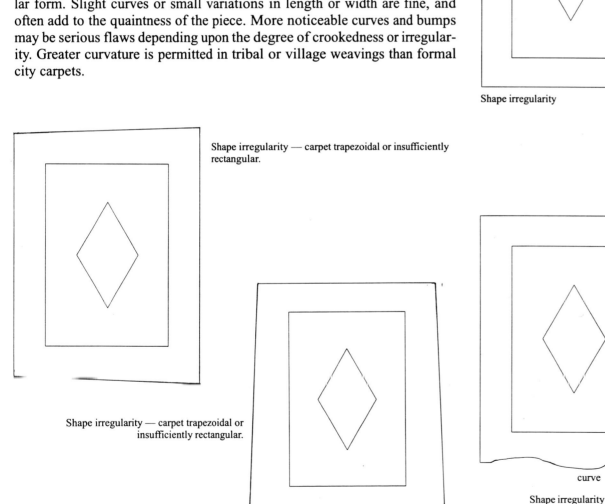

Shape irregularity — carpet trapezoidal or insufficiently rectangular.

Shape irregularity — carpet trapezoidal or insufficiently rectangular.

bump

curve

Shape irregularity

curve

Shape irregularity

Design Irregularities

Sometimes designs are not perfectly symmetrical because the weaver did not execute the plan, cartoon, or diagram precisely. Often the imperfection is manifested when the center medallion is several inches closer to one border than the other. Or, one border may be three or four inches wider than the border on the opposite side. In either case, one or two inches can be forgiven, but three or more inches may be troubling. Normally, the smaller the rug, the less design disproportion is tolerable. Rarely, one or more weavers might change the entire design in the beginning, middle, or end of the carpet. This blemish is frequently quite serious, particularly when found in city or town rugs.

These imbalances should not be confused with the spontaneous creativity and squashed or elongated medallions characteristic of many great antique nomadic and village carpets. These changes are merely ways in which the weaver expresses her individuality in the midst of the symmetry and repetitiveness of this traditional art form. The permutations are not flaws and add to the beauty and quaintness of the piece.

Symmetry has been significantly disrupted in many new natural dyed Turkish village rugs, and the resulting variations have evolved into a new art form under the aegis of certain Western producers. Weavers may be puzzled and confused as they craft pieces with so much disharmony, but asymmetry may be slowly becoming part of the cognitive map of the craftswomen in Eastern Turkey and other parts of the Orient. These experimental weavings sometimes complement modern room decoration better than traditional symmetrical carpets.

Although design and color imbalance is fashionable in the West today, unbridled experimentation is sometimes excessive. There should be a certain degree of order, equilibrium, or calmness in rugs. Patterns and hues may be somewhat irregular, but the piece must not be a confused mass of disorder with beautiful, highly variegated, dyes. More asymmetry may be accepted in more unstructured carpets but there must be an overall harmony of design and color wherein sundry imbalances are manifested. People generally shy away from rugs that are too carelessly drawn and dyed.

Sometimes the designs may be symmetrical but the colors in one or two motifs are not balanced. This color asymmetry is a rare but significant imperfection that is probably more serious in formal city carpets than in informal tribal and village weavings.

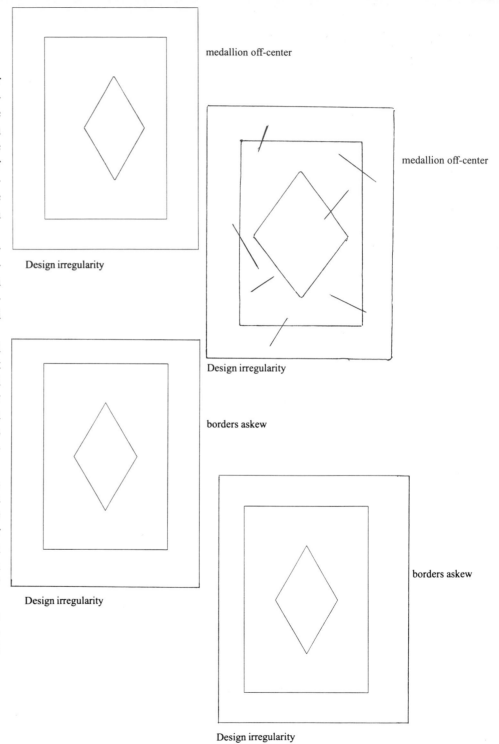

medallion off-center

Design irregularity

medallion off-center

Design irregularity

borders askew

Design irregularity

borders askew

Design irregularity

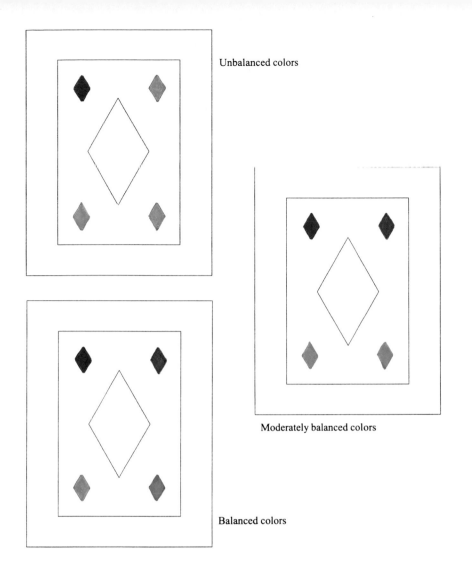

Unbalanced colors

Moderately balanced colors

Balanced colors

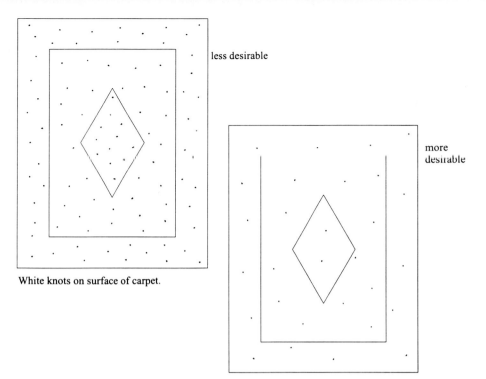

less desirable

more desirable

White knots on surface of carpet.

White knots on surface of carpet.

Visible Knots

Sometimes unsightly white knots appear on the surface of the rug where there should be pile. They are at times found in semi-antique Kerman and Nichols Chinese carpets as well as fine antique Kashan rugs. They may also be present in other pieces. White knots do not represent a flaw if there are not too many in the weaving. However, the value of the rug may be slightly reduced if these specks are pervasive. In order to avoid weakening the foundation, they should preferably be left alone or simply touched up, but not cut out, or even pushed through, the carpet by the dealer. These knots are part of the natural weaving process and are usually the result of tying horizontal cotton weft threads of various lengths to one another throughout the rug.

Oxidization

Sometimes certain antique rugs contain black or brownish black dyes that are made from substances that disintegrate wool over time. As the wool corrodes and disappears an embossed effect results when adjacent piled areas are highlighted by the missing nap. These oxidized areas appear to be worn but the yarn has simply eroded naturally. Oxidization is not a very serious flaw, and the areas devoid of black dyed wool can be filled in perfectly with the same colored yarn by a restorer. Russian Shirvan, Turkish Yoruk, Persian Kurdish, and many other carpets occasionally manifest this phenomenon.

Deep pomegranate and garnet red dyes that are often found in old Indian Agra and Amritsar carpets may also corrode wool.

Certain new natural dyed Turkish rugs have higher definition in their designs because black wool was sheared to the foundation either for aesthetic reasons or to replicate the look of oxidized back wool found in some antique carpets. The procedure of clipping black yarn by hand is terribly risky and has thankfully been reduced in recent years. The integrity of the rug may be damaged when adjacent wool in other colors is accidentally cut away, or if black nap is incompletely sheared.

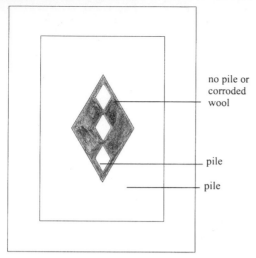

no pile or corroded wool

pile

pile

Oxidization, or localized areas where brownish-black or black colored wool has naturally disintegrated.

Touchup

Many old carpets are touched up and this contingency is not an impeachable offense. However, dealers generally don't buy painted rugs, and prestigious auction houses normally won't accept them. One may rub a small spot on the worn surface with a damp white handkerchief to see if color is removed. If the dye appears on the cloth, the rug was probably painted. If one can buy a carpet before it has been touched up and repaired, and if one is able to tolerate the uneven condition, the resale value of the rug will be higher. One may arrange furniture to cover holes and worn areas, or put damaged sections in low trafficked areas. Some fine designers favor the look of old, evenly worn pieces in fairly rough condition with white caps or spots where the nap has been lost.

Most people prefer their rugs serviced and hopefully the vendor has good painters and restorers. The touch up artist should use a special quill-like pen and match the ink color to the wool exactly. He must touch up only those spots where the nap is missing. These specks, or white caps, are points where the wool is worn down, or where no pile remains. He should follow the abrash or subtle changes in the original wool color as closely as possible. A good painter will not paint more than absolutely necessary, and if he does a good job, following the design exactly with precisely matched colors, the piece may be a fine purchase even if some of it is touched up. Worn rugs with wool warps and wefts such as certain Bidjars, Afghans, and Shirazes cannot be tinted because the dyes will not adhere to wool.

If one purchases a painted carpet, one should arrange for the vendor to clean and service it in the future, if possible.

The surface and back of many rust-colored carpets, such as Sarouks, imported to the United States about seventy years ago, were completely painted to attain the fashionable red hue. Painted Sarouks were especially popular in America for many years. Today these rugs often have blotchy colors because some of the paint has been lost after successive washings. Dealers usually have the red color stripped and the original rust color reduced to a beautiful pale salmon shade. Stripping is normally, but not always, successful, and there are always risks involved in the removal of colors. Although the foundation may be slightly weakened by the chemicals used in the process, the carpet will be far more salable. Stripping is a very important part of the antique Sarouk trade. These lightened carpets are generally sold to Italy, if worn, or Germany, if in excellent condition. If one wishes to have a touched up Sarouk stripped, one should contact a reputable carpet cleaner with the facilities to handle the task.

Color Run

Color run is a major flaw and rugs with even a little bleeding of one dye into another should, in general, be avoided. Most dealers do not buy carpets with color run. A small amount of bleeding often indicates that the fugitive dye pervades the entire piece. Color run on the fringes of red Afgan and other rugs is usually not very serious. Red and blue occasionally run into ivory and carpets should be closely examined for this problem. Ivory or white wool should be clear and not even slightly tinged with red, blue, or any other color. A little fugitive red dye can often be successfully removed with certain chemicals found in rug supply stores, but these fugitive dyes should generally be left untreated because there is always a danger of bleaching adjacent colors.

Old carpets that have recently been painted and new rugs whose dyes have not been adequately tested for color fastness, should probably not be washed for a few years to let the colors settle in the wool.

The more extraordinary the carpet the more forgiving one might be about a little color run. Very rare and important antique Agra rugs, with tightly packed knots, sometimes have a slight degree of bleeding, but this imperfection does not seriously affect their value.

Stains

Immediately blot all stains with a dry tissue or paper towel and then wipe with a sponge dampened with water or club soda. Stains may also be cleaned with a damp sponge and a little mild detergent. The detergent should be gently wiped out of the carpet with a water-dampened sponge. Most minor stains can be removed or at least diluted and should come out in the next cleaning. Or one may saturate the stain with an effective spray solvent and blot with a paper towel. Stain removers are frequently found in hardware, carpet supply, or vacuum repair stores. A few surface spots on antique weavings are not as worrisome as larger blemishes visible on both sides of the rug.

One should consult a reliable carpet cleaner for specific chemical mixtures to remove particularly bad stains. The entire rug may have to be promptly taken to a cleaner if damaged by flooding, burst pipes, or unusual staining. Experienced carpet cleaners can remove many stains with sufficient time.

People who own dogs should take great care of their carpets because dealers, in general, do not buy animal-stained rugs. Dog urine damages both dyes and foundation and the proper stain removing solution must be immediately applied. Dog lovers should either buy only inexpensive or machine-made carpets, or remove stains diligently, and send rugs to the cleaners more frequently. Ivory, or lighter colored yarns, may not be as noticeably affected by dog stains, or the chemicals used in the removal of such blemishes, as darker fibers. Cats with sharp claws may churn up and twist the pile and damage fringes, but usually do not stain carpets, if properly trained.

People who are not meticulous should avoid buying rugs with open-field designs that readily show stains. They must also have carpets cleaned more frequently because stains sometimes cannot be completely blotted out and washed away with a sponge and water. Acids from residual stains hidden beneath the surface of the pile will often damage the dyes over time. Laymen are usually shocked by the color losses, light areas, and streaking that result from rubbing stains into the wool, and then cleaning the rug many years later. They sometimes incorrectly blame the cleaner for these unusual and unexpected forms of discoloration, a mistake old carpet dealers rarely make because they expect the worst when very dirty rugs are commercially washed.

Because so many rugs are returned to dealers after they have been tried at home, they often become slightly soiled. This dirt is unimportant and can easily be washed off with soap and water by the merchant; however, if the grime cannot be completely removed, one should not buy the carpet.

Rug owners should generally wear slippers in the house because sweat from feet may cause color loss in sections of the carpet that are continuously exposed to perspiration. Discoloration usually occurs in areas adjacent to the bed or sofa.

Fringe and Selvedge Wear

Wear often begins on the heavily trafficked borders, but the fringes, or ends of the warps which run up and down the length of the carpet, are usually the first part of the fabric to wear out. Edges or selvedges along the sides of the rug frequently weaken and unravel a little later. One should closely inspect these areas from time to time to see if repair or overcasting is required. Overcasting is an inexpensive procedure in which a line of thread is hand-sewn around areas of the ends and selvedges that are in jeopardy of losing knots. This stitching may be done by restorers at the cleaning facility when the rug is washed. If you are careful, you can prevent the development of serious fringe and edge wear.

Artificial or added fringes sewn onto the ends of the carpet are sometimes a sign of the loss of a few lines of adjacent knots, a fairly serious flaw. They may be the equivalent of a bandaid that covers a more serious wound. The complete repair could be an expensive procedure that involves the extension of the real fringes and rebuilding of the outer guard borders. A "sanjure," or row of knots sewn onto the end of the rug to prevent further unraveling, may also be needed. In general, attached fringes are an unnecessary and unsightly addition to a carpet because they serve no important purpose and may clash with the rest of the piece. Pile loss on the ends may signify that other areas of the carpet are worn.

The bright, white cotton fringes on new rugs should be left alone and not darkened with tea or other substances. They will darken with time.

New selvedges are not a serious imperfection if they match the color, fineness, and delicacy of the carpet, and no rows of knots have been lost. A fairly serious flaw results if a few lines of knots are missing in a solid color and a major imperfection arises if several rows are absent and designs are lost or incomplete. One should examine the patterns and rows of knots beside the edges of the piece and compare them with the complete ends to determine how much of the sides have been lost and the significance of this defect.

On rare occasions, bad wool from dead sheep is used for the warps of certain rugs. If one gently pulls a thread from the fringe, the wool splits apart because it is inelastic or weak. The carpet should not be purchased because it probably will not last long or survive a commercial cleaning.

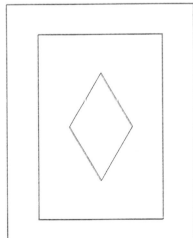

Dog stains that can damage dyes and foundation of carpet.

Lighter colored areas and streaking that results from dye loss when old stains are removed by commercial cleaning.

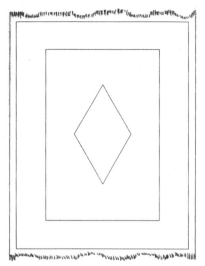

Wear and fringe loss along both ends of carpet.

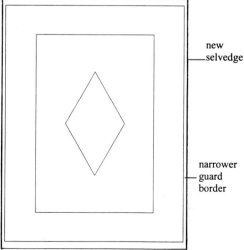

added fringe

Artificial fringes sewn onto carpet and loss of a few rows of knots on ends.

narrower guard border

Wear and selvedge loss along both edges of carpet.

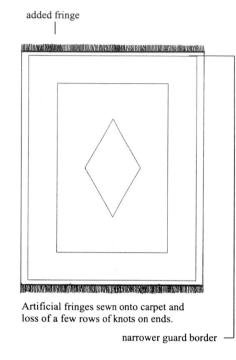

new selvedge

narrower guard border

New selvedges sewn onto carpet and loss of a few rows of knots on edges.

Repair

Finding a good restorer is always difficult. The best tend to be especially expensive and the mediocre are inconsistent. In general, the dearer the cost of the repair the better the result so it is hard to comparison shop for a restorer. Good repair work was always costly in the past and is even more expensive today so expect to pay more than one might think is appropriate. It is best not to scrimp on restoring a good piece.

A repair may be quite good and a client may believe it is bad or a poor restoration may be overappreciated. For example, a hole is usually somewhat round but the restorer may cut a small area of carpet around it in the shape of a square. A little loom is now made and a miniature rug is woven where the hole was situated. The pile on the repair is slightly higher than the rest of the piece so the knots will not fall out, and the restored area will flatten over time and meld with the rest of the carpet. So a small square rewoven area with a slightly higher pile may be an excellent repair, but a client might think it is not well done.

Repairs should not be made unless absolutely necessary in order to maintain the integrity of the rug. Holes that have been stitched up and are not in danger of splitting open should probably be left alone. Selvedges should only be replaced if they cannot be expeditiously salvaged. Worn areas can often be protected by adding wool to the surface of the carpet. This non-invasive cashmere embroidery is known as "khav."

A restoration should closely resemble the design, color, and texture of the rest of the rug but will never match perfectly, despite certain age-old remedies used by the repairer to blend it with the rest of the carpet, such as slight staining with tea, or singeing with a flame.

A reliable old carpet dealer should be contacted to see if a rug merits repair. The vast majority of dealers are objective in the performance of this valuable service, which should not cost too much money. The dealer should be able to recommend a restorer that is honest, reliable, and competent, and other dealers may be asked for their opinions. Good repairers are often found in used carpet centers where they work for many dealers in the trade. They are usually busy but accept work from private clients. One must be patient as a good restoration takes time. Major repair should not be done at cleaning facilities because they generally do not have qualified restorers capable of handling difficult jobs at a fair price. Antique and semi-antique Chinese rugs should preferably not be repaired because it is almost impossible to match the colors of the yarns.

Purchasing a carpet with restoration is also problematical. Study the surface of the pile to see if an area of irregular texture, color, or design is present. Turn the rug over to find out if a small area of knots is slightly different in appearance from the rest of the piece. Unfortunately, it is difficult for the

184

layman to tell if the condition is good, and ideally the carpet is in perfect shape, full piled, without restoration. Better condition is more likely in finely woven traditional rugs such as Kermans, Sarouks, Kashans, and Indias than more loosely woven decorative pieces such as Mahals, Herizes, Serapes, and Oushaks, but great care must be taken in examining all old carpets.

In general, do not buy carpets in poor condition with large rewoven areas of more than one and one half inches in diameter. Also, avoid carpets with extensive moth damage, dry rot, color run, excessive touchup on more than twenty percent of the piece, alterations, or any other major flaws. If the rug one is considering has a little moth damage, it should ideally not have any other imperfections. If it has some touchup, it should preferably not have any repairs. Most dealers follow the proviso, "Two strikes and you're out" with regard to a carpet's imperfections. Superficial wear is not as significant as the complete loss of nap on the front and back of the rug. One must try to be as fastidious as possible when inspecting an old carpet. Semi-antique weavings, about forty to sixty years old, are usually in better condition than antique rugs and may be a safer purchase.

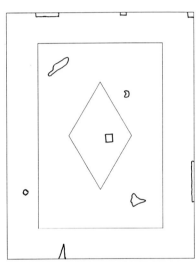

Repair, or areas of new pile woven into carpet.

Semi-antique pieces often lack the beauty, patina, and open design of older carpets, but they are generally less expensive, and only a few years away from becoming antiques. They are also more frequently purchased by old rug wholesalers today. Try to find examples without the bright, obtrusive colors commonly found in many Persian and Turkish carpets from the early to middle part of the twentieth century.

Patches

Carpets with large damaged areas often require patches because repair would be too costly. Dealers and repairers usually have boxes filled with patches or small pieces of carpet in various sizes and shapes

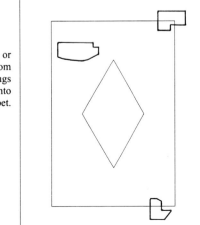

Patches, or pieces from other rugs sewn into carpet.

garnered from cannibalized rugs. Good patches are scarce today, but if a patch can be found that closely approximates the pile, design, and color of the carpet in need of repair, the result may be almost as good as a restoration, and much less expensive; however, the cost of a good patch that is correctly sewn into the rug has gone up in recent years. One should be patient and allow the restorer plenty of time to find the proper patch as this service generally takes a while.

Cut and Reduced

When a piece of fabric is removed along the entire width or length of the rug, a most significant flaw results. A section is more often cut out from the length than the width before the carpet is rejoined again. The rug is frequently reduced in two places along the inner guard borders or edges of the main field in order to maintain symmetry. The carpet is usually expertly sewn back together in a stepped manner so that the pattern closely resembles the original design of the rug. It is often difficult for an expert to tell if a carpet has been reduced or altered so it is particularly hard for the layman to notice this extremely serious imperfection. It is always a good idea to turn the piece over to see if any thick, unusual, and frequently staggered lines or seams are running horizontally from edge to edge or vertically from end to end. On the face one might see incomplete flowers or a truncated medallion, or one may find that one half of the rug, usually running lengthwise, is shorter than the other.

A carpet is generally diminished in size in order to remove a badly worn or damaged area. Occasionally a rug is reduced to fit a room. The value of a cut carpet is significantly less than one that is complete, and altered rugs should generally be avoided. The vendor should guarantee in writing that the piece has not been dininished in size. Dealers rarely buy cut carpets.

The loss of part or all of the outer guard borders, or main borders, is sometimes the result of altering the rug to fit a room. Normally these very serious losses are also the consequence of wear. Missing main borders or sections from the body of the rug might be the equivalent of an antique table with shortened legs. Beautiful old carpets that contain either of these imperfections are often in excellent condition otherwise, and suspiciously less expensive than expected. A stunning, full-piled antique Kerman in an odd 9 x 10 foot size that retails for only $8,000 should raise an eyebrow and inspire one to inspect it very closely.

The loss of a few rows of knots on the ends of important antique Persian Herizes and Serapes is becoming a little more acceptable in the trade because of the increased scarcity of these rugs.

If a section is removed to accommodate a fireplace and then resewn back into the carpet, a flaw also results, but this imperfection is not as serious as one in which the rug is altered and an entire section is lost.

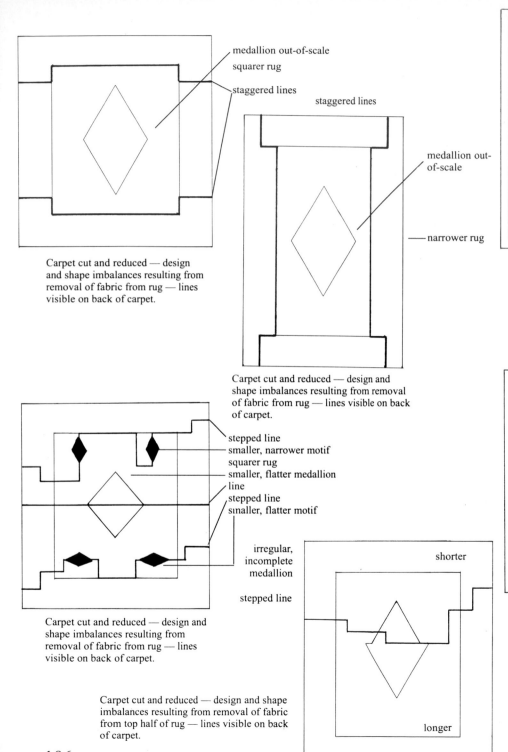

medallion out-of-scale

squarer rug

staggered lines

Carpet cut and reduced — design and shape imbalances resulting from removal of fabric from rug — lines visible on back of carpet.

staggered lines

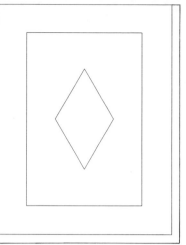

medallion out-of-scale

— narrower rug

Carpet cut and reduced — design and shape imbalances resulting from removal of fabric from rug — lines visible on back of carpet.

stepped line
smaller, narrower motif
squarer rug
smaller, flatter medallion
line
stepped line
smaller, flatter motif

irregular, incomplete medallion

stepped line

Carpet cut and reduced — design and shape imbalances resulting from removal of fabric from rug — lines visible on back of carpet.

Carpet cut and reduced — design and shape imbalances resulting from removal of fabric from top half of rug — lines visible on back of carpet.

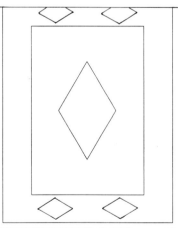

shorter

longer

guard border

Guard border missing on one end of carpet — usually the result of wear.

guard border

Guard borders missing on both edges of carpet — usually the result of wear.

motif incomplete

guard border

Guard border missing and main border incomplete on one end of carpet — usually the result of wear.

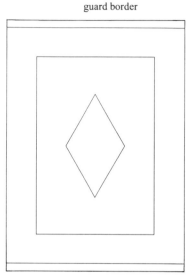

guard border

motif incomplete

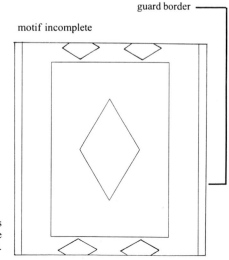

Guard borders missing and main borders incomplete on both ends of carpet — usually the result of wear.

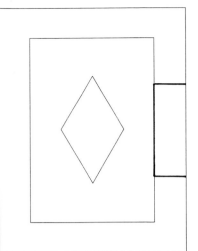

Fireplace section resewn into carpet after removal — lines visible on back of rug.

Sometimes a carpet will not lie flat on the floor or has bumps that do not flatten with use. This problem may be caused by unequal loom tension during weaving, which results in excess fabric in certain areas, usually the borders. In order to remedy this imperfection, and prevent foldwear, the rug is cut, excess carpet is removed, and the area is resewn. The result is a visible line or seam on the back of the piece, an irregular pattern on the front, and the loss of a small amount of pile. This line or wrinkle may be a few inches or several feet in length and is always a serious flaw. In general, one should try to avoid rugs that have been cut and joined to make them lie flat. People who own antique Kazaks or other carpets with foldwear, or thick lines that are devoid of pile, should not cut the fissures out unless they are splitting apart.

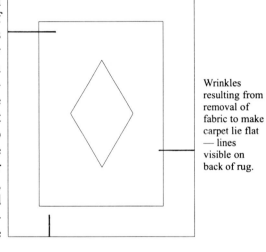

Wrinkles resulting from removal of fabric to make carpet lie flat — lines visible on back of rug.

A little lumpiness, common in carpets with wool warps, is not serious because the piece will usually flatten with padding and use.

Dry Rot

Finely woven traditional rugs are more susceptible to dry rot than loosely woven decorative weavings. This extremely serious imperfection is manifested when the cotton warps and wefts that are tightly packed against one another lose their elasticity, become brittle, and eventually turn to powder and disintegrate. This decay of the foundation represents the death of the carpet.

Merchants gently bend or fold the rug, and if the back cracks, dry rot is present, and may pervade the entire piece. Because dry-rotted carpets crack easily, they are often rolled inside out with the pile exposed in order to prevent breaks and splits in the foundation. A piece that is rolled inside out in a dealer's showroom may be brittle. If dry rot is advanced, extensive splitting and cracking occurs on the back of the rug. In order to maintain the integrity of the carpet, repairers must sew all the little splits together. There are tricks that dealers use to restore moisture and elasticity to the rug, but these improvements are usually short-lived.

Dry rot is generally invisible, but diminishes value significantly, and dealers normally do not buy carpets that have this form of deterioration. The piece may be in excellent condition on the surface, with perfect pile, and still suffer from the defect.

Certain antique Agra and Amritsar rugs, with many splits, cracks, and tears sewn together throughout the carpet, may also have dry rot.

The flaw often develops most egregiously in the area beneath or around a flower pot. Dry rot usually occurs when the plant is in a basket and water overlaps the dish beneath the pot onto the rug. The warps and wefts that are continuously exposed to dampness become hard and eventually dry and brittle. This area is difficult to repair because the damaged area must be cut out to where the foundation is strong and healthy prior to rebuilding and reweaving. Most carpets would not merit the costs involved in reweaving an area twelve inches or more in diameter. Flower pots that are placed on rugs should never be put in baskets and great care must be taken to prevent exposure of the weaving to dampness. It is necessary to move flower pots to different locations periodically.

Humidifiers should not be set directly on the carpet and must also be relocated from time to time.

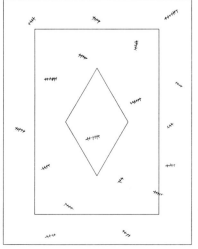

advanced disintegration of foundation

Dry Rot — splits and cracks sewn together on back of carpet.

187

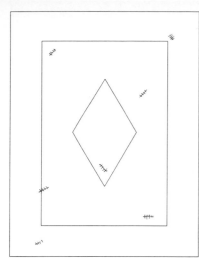

moderate disintegration of foundation

Dry Rot — splits and cracks sewn together on back of carpet.

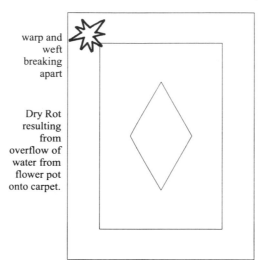

warp and weft breaking apart

Dry Rot resulting from overflow of water from flower pot onto carpet.

Moth Damage

Moths are the bane of the carpet business and a very serious problem for dealers who must spend a lot of time and money periodically fumigating their inventories. Merchants usually do not buy rugs that have more than a small amount of moth damage. Pile loss sometimes occurs because the fleece was inadequately washed prior to dying. This affliction is manifested by missing wool in areas where pile is full, and tiny, but noticeable, larva, or stringy white cotton-like organisms, about half an inch in length, throughout the piece. When the small larvae is peeled off with the fingernail a little bit of carpet goes with it. The longer the larva remain on the rug the more nap will be lost. If one sees any very thin, thread-like substances on the front or back of the carpet, immediately wipe them away with a fairly soft nylon brush. If the moth presence is superficial, a cleaning may not be necessary.

Advanced destruction on the back of the weaving is exhibited by white areas of bare warp threads uncovered by the wool knots that have been ravaged.

When the damaged areas are repaired, the colors and wool texture will not match the rest of the rug perfectly. The colors found in an old restoration may be lighter than the rest of the carpet because they tend to fade more rapidly than the original dyes after successive washings.

Moth damage is more likely to develop in lightly trafficked sections that lie fallow for long periods. Parts of rugs that lie underneath sofas, cabinets, or dressers are particularly vulnerable and should be vacuumed periodically,

at least several times a year if possible. Ends, selvedges, and borders are therefore often attacked first, and a little damage in one area is usually a sign of more devastation throughout the piece. Moth flakes or napthalane may occasionally be lightly sprinkled over and under fabric that lies beneath couches, side tables, or bookcases.

Storing carpets, rolled up or folded, for many years, is a recipe for disaster. Pieces not in use should be protected with moth balls or flakes (napthalene) and occasionally opened, lightly brushed, vacuumed, and exposed to air and light for a little while. The back of the rug may be lightly sprayed with Lysol. Moth balls or flakes in fairly generous quantities can be thrown on the front and back of the carpet prior to rolling or folding. Do not roll too tightly or place heavy weight on folded pieces because staining from napthalene may occur. Napthalene is highly toxic so one must minimize exposure to it. Flakes are probably superior to balls because they are easier to apply evenly, cover more surface area, and penetrate the pile more deeply. They are less likely to stain than balls because they disintegrate more rapidly, and are more effective for protecting kilims.

If there is a lot of moth damage, the piece may be beyond repair and should perhaps be discarded. An old rug dealer may be consulted to see if the carpet merits restoration. It is sometimes difficult for the dealer to determine if repair is warranted because he cannot know exactly how much pile will be lost during the cleaning. If the rug is important, or of high sentimental value, it is usually worth the price of a cleaning to find out how much remains intact.

Afghan carpets, with their inadequately washed, greasy wool, are frequently at high risk for moth development and should be vacuumed and cleaned with great regularity. Chemically washed rugs are less susceptible to moths but must still be protected with napthalene.

Sprays that kill moths are available in large amounts from carpet supply stores and smaller quantities can probably be purchased from old rug dealers. Padding, vacuuming, rotation, and cleaning reduce the likelihood of damage and are essential to carpet care.

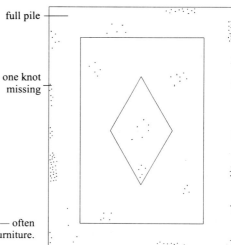

full pile

one knot missing

Missing pile resulting from moth damage — often found in areas that lie beneath furniture.

Carpet Care

Padding

Padding is always beneficial to carpets. Many excellent synthetic rubber brands are available from rug supply stores and carpet retailers. Non-slip pads are quite thin and have a spongy mesh structure with air pockets. They are very popular and can be used for both pile and flat woven rugs. Thicker synthetic felt padding may be used for antique carpets, thinner kilims, and needlepoints to soften the feeling underfoot. Any good pad should prevent the rug from slipping on hardwood or smooth surfaces while not staining the back of the carpet or floor. Padding also helps the rug lie flat, increases longevity by reducing friction, and diminishes the likelihood of moth damage by creating more hygienic conditions between the carpet and floor.

If an area rug is placed on a broadloom carpet, a thin adhesive padding should be placed in between to prevent buckling and slippage. The fibers on the back of the scatter rug may be damaged by friction if the buffer is not present. This sticky, sheer padding is usually available in carpet supply stores.

Double-faced tape, available in most hardware stores, may be used around the edges of the rug to cleave the fabric to the floor if padding is inadequate. Elderly or wheelchair bound people should preferably use adhesive tape instead of gluing or nailing a valuable carpet to the floor.

Vacuuming

Vacuuming is probably more important for the prevention of moth development than the cleaning of dirt. The back of the rug should be vigorously vacuumed periodically and the front cleaned at least twice a month, if possible. Vacuum the delicate fringes and selvedges more gently. Quick Brooms of six amperes are fine and the cleaner does not have to be too powerful. A cleaner of four amperes is sufficient for kilims or flat weaves. Beating the back of scatter rugs, a venerable tradition in Europe, is an excellent way to shake out embedded dirt.

A slightly dampened sponge may be used to wipe off wool that sheds from the surface of the nap. Gently wipe in the direction of the pile.

The loss of a certain amount of wool from the face of the pile is quite common and does not signify that weak, inferior, or inelastic wool has been used; however, if an excessive amount of yarn can easily be brushed away by rubbing, the best wool may not have been used in the construction of the carpet.

Because some professional cleaning plants do not adequately remove dust, rugs should be thoroughly vacuumed, front and back if possible, before being sent to wash. Old, densely packed carpets, such as seventy-year-old Sarouks, that have been neglected for many years, often need to be vacuumed by dealers with powerful cleaners ten to twenty times, front and back, until no dust remains on the floor.

Rug Rotation

The single most important action that must be taken to preserve the life of a carpet is to rotate it 180 degrees regularly. This may be done every few years or after cleaning. The location of all scatter rugs should be changed periodically. The purpose is to prevent excessive wear in areas that are heavily trafficked and promote even sunfading. Rotation helps avert wear and discoloration from staining that commonly occurs in the area between the sofa and coffee table.

Sometimes valuable carpets are not rotated for twenty years or more. If they had been turned even once within that time period their value might have increased considerably.

Rugs should not be exposed to excessive sun. Blinds or curtains may be used to disperse and diminish the light. In order to avoid uneven sunfading, often a serious imperfection if too much color is lost, carpets that are exposed to a lot of sunlight must be rotated more frequently, or at least once a year, if possible. Rotation will also prevent dark areas from developing in parts of a rug that lie beneath furniture. Hopefully the piece will fade evenly and there will be no need to tint areas where the colors have been bleached by the sun. Ivory or very light colored carpets will probably be less affected by strong sunlight than medium to dark hued rugs.

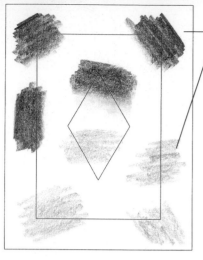

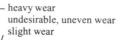
heavy wear
undesirable, uneven wear
slight wear

Wear, or areas where no pile remains on surface of carpet.

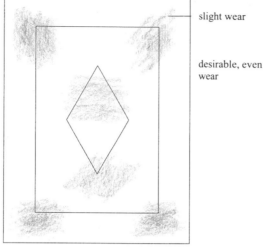
slight wear

desirable, even wear

Wear, or areas where no pile remains on surface of carpet.

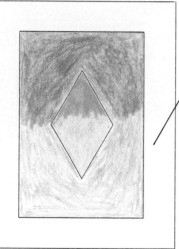
faded, lighter colored area

Sunfading, or colors bleached by sunlight.

faded, lighter colored area

Uneven fading — darkened areas of carpet that lie beneath furniture

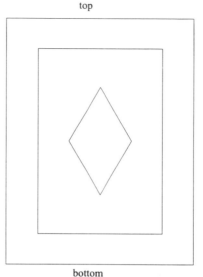
top

bottom

Rotation, or turning carpet around 180 degrees.

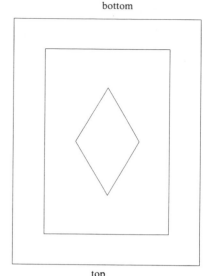
bottom

top

Rotation, or turning carpet around 180 degrees.

Cleaning

Carpets must be cleaned about every three years to remove stains, prevent moth damage, promote even wear, further color maturity, and foster the development of a patina or surface sheen. Cleaning protects dyes and fibers by diminishing the dust, dirt, and grime embedded in the wool. Most reputable carpet cleaners will know how to safely wash different types of rugs.

Extra care should be taken with old fragile carpets, delicate new weavings, and rugs of high sentimental value. A reputable professional cleaner, with several years of experience and the proper equipment, should be able to handle all types of problems, including stains and fringe or selvedge wear. Sometimes a small plant with a knowledgeable owner of integrity can give excellent personal service, but generally large, established facilities are safer and have better beating and rinsing machines for the essential removal of dust and dirt. A few less reputable cleaners may try to buy important pieces from clients without solicitation. Although carpets are normally picked up at the home by the cleaner, one may wish to take an important piece in person to the plant to check the facilities and discuss stain removal and methods of cleaning.

If one is conscientious and finds a reliable cleaner, one should be able to obviate the necessity of a costly conservatory wash. Even carpets that are quite expensive and delicate may be cleaned confidently and inexpensively at the right facility. The plant should also have the capacity to dry clean needlepoints, Aubussons, and kilims.

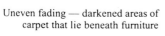

Different commercial cleaners may have slightly divergent methods, but the process of professional cleaning normally involves several steps beginning with dust removal in a beating machine or drum. After the dust is removed, both sides of the piece are soap scrubbed on the floor with a brush or power jet machine. Then the rug is rinsed completely with an automatic cleansing machine and wrung when squeezed through rollers. Finally it is hung from a high ceiling in a hot room, under controlled temperatures, to dry quickly, and prevent color run. The carpet is inspected, rolled, and wrapped in paper before being returned.

Another method of washing old or delicate rugs and even more durable weavings is to take them to a reputable used carpet dealer. After a thorough vacuuming with a powerful machine, the dealer will then use a round soap injecting machine to clean the piece on the floor. This is a safe method that yields a fairly deep cleaning, but not all the soap will be extracted by the machine. Old painted rugs can be carefully monitored as colors sometimes wash out during the process. The dealer can then retouch those areas in need of attention. Some merchants wash painted pieces with a dilute vinegar solution.

Carpets without significant stains may be cleaned at home if one has sufficient space. A small rug or kilim should be vacuumed and washed with a mild fabric cleanser such as dilute Woolite or soap. It can be sponge washed by hand in the bath tub or on a cement or linoleum floor, front and back, using a circular motion. It may be rinsed in cold water, soaked in the tub for a little while, and then thoroughly rinsed again until the dirt and soap are removed. It must then be dried as quickly as possible to prevent color run and prolonged moisturization of the foundation. Any objects that will not stain the rug such as plastic baskets, chairs, and flower pots, should be placed under the piece to allow air to circulate and speed drying. The carpet should dry in about a day or two depending upon the humidity. The pile might at first be twisted and lumpy, but will become flatter and smoother with use.

Follow a similar procedure for a large carpet which may be washed outside the house in the driveway. If one does not have a soap injecting and rinsing machine, one may gently rinse with a hose, front and back, and again place objects underneath to facilitate drying.

Remember to lay the rug in the other direction in the room to promote even wear.

If one does not commonly wear slippers in the house, a rough, heavy, and thick mat made of sisal, hemp, or jute should be placed outside the front and back doors on which to wipe the soles of shoes.

Carpet Savers

It is always a good idea to use plastic cups or rug savers under furniture legs to prevent the crushing and wearing of the pile. They are particularly useful in dispersing the weight of heavy wrought iron tables that can damage the nap quite easily. It is also important to move furniture an inch or two from time to time to avoid mashing the wool. Lighter weight furniture with legs that can readily be lifted and shifted is often preferred for easier carpet care. If the legs remain in the same position year after year, particularly without rug savers, the nap may never spring back even after cleaning, and the unsightly spots will have to be filled in or repiled. The value of the carpet will be reduced.

Bibliography

Bennett, Ian (ed.). *Complete Illustrated Rugs and Carpets of the World.* New York: A&W Publishers, Inc., 1977.

Black, David (ed.). *The MacMillan Atlas of Rugs & Carpets.* New York: MacMillan Publishing Company, 1985.

Eiland, Murray L. *Oriental Rugs: A New Comprehensive Guide.* Boston: Little, Brown and Company, 1981.

Ford, P.R.J. *The Oriental Carpet: A History and Guide to Traditional Motifs, Patterns, and Symbols.* 1981. Reprint. New York: Portland House, 1989.

Glassie, Henry. *Turkish Traditional Art Today.* Bloomington: Indiana University Press, 1993.

Hawley, Walter A. *Oriental Rugs, Antique and Modern.* 1913. Reprint. New York: Dover Publications, Inc., 1970.

Mumford, John Kimberly. *Oriental Rugs.* 1929. Reprint. New York: Clarkson N. Potter, 1981.

Opie, James. *Tribal Rugs of Southern Persia.* Portland: James Opie Oriental Rugs, Inc., 1981.

Petsopoulos, Yanni. *Kilims, Masterpieces From Turkey.* New York: Rizzoli International Publications, Inc., 1991.

Purdon, Nicholas. *Carpet and Textile Patterns.* London: Laurence King Publishing, 1996.

Thompson, Jon. *Oriental Carpets.* New York: Penguin Books USA Inc., 1993.

Appendix

Old Carpets Commonly Found in the Trade

Generic Name	Origin	Geo-metric	Floral	Repeat Medallion	Center Medallion	Overall	Size	Quality
Afghan	Afghanistan	+		+		+	R	M to F
Afshar	Iran	+		+	+	+	S	M
Agra	India	+	+		+	+	R	F
Amritsar	India		+		+		R	F
Aubusson	France	+	+	+	+	+	R	F
Bakshaiash	Iran	+			+	+	R-S	C to M
Baktiari	Iran	+			+	+	R-S	M
Belouch	I-A-B	+				+	S	M
Bergama	Turkey	+		+	+		S	C to M
Beshir	Turkestan	+	+			+	R-S	M
Bibikabad	Iran	+	+		+	+	R-S	C to M
Bidjar	Iran	+	+		+	+	R-S	M to F
Chinese-Peking	China	+	+		+	+	R-S	C
Chinese-Nichols	China	+	+			+	R-S	C to M
Ferahan	Iran	+	+		+	+	R-S	F
Hamadan	Iran	+	+		+	+	R-S	C to M
Heriz	Iran	+			+	+	R-S	C to M
India	India		+			+	R	F
Isfahan	Iran		+		+	+	R-S	F
Kashan	Iran		+		+	+	R-S	F
Karabagh	Caucasus	+				+	Runner-K	M
Kazak	Caucasus	+		+			S	M
Kazvin	Iran		+		+	+	R-S	M
Kilim-Bessarabian	Europe	+			+	+	S	F
Kilim-Senneh	Iran	+	+		+	+	S	F
Kilim-Shirvan	Caucasus	+		+		+	S	F
Kilim-Turkish	Turkey	+		+	+	+	R-S	F
Kerman	Iran		+		+	+	R-S	F

Generic Name	Origin	Geo-metric	Floral	Repeat Medallion	Center Medallion	Overall	Size	Quality
Khotan	East Turkestan	+	+			+	R-S	C to M
Kurdish	Iran	+				+	S	C to M
Lillihan	Iran		+		+	+	R-S	M
Malayer	Iran	+			+	+	R-S	M
Mahal	Iran	+	+		+	+	R-S	C to M
Meshed	Iran		+		+	+	R	F
Needlepoint	Europe	+	+	+	+	+	R-S	F
Oushak	Turkey	+			+	+	R	C
Qashqai	Iran	+		+	+		S	F
Qum	Iran		+		+	+	S	F
Serab	Iran	+		+			Runner-K	M
Sarouk	Iran		+		+	+	R-S	M to F
Savonnerie	Europe	+	+		+	+	R	C
Senneh	Iran	+	+		+	+	R-S	F
Serape	Iran	+			+		R-S	C to M
Serabend	Iran	+	+			+	K	M
Shirvan	Caucasus	+		+		+	S	M to F
Shiraz	Iran	+		+	+		S	M
Sivas	Turkey	+	+		+	+	R-S	M to F
Spanish	Spain	+		+		+	R-S	C
Soumak	Caucasus	+		+			R-S	F
Sultanabad	Iran	+			+	+	R	C to M
Tabriz	Iran	+	+		+	+	R-S	M to F
Turkish	Turkey	+	+	+	+	+	R-S	C to F
Turkoman	Turkmen-istan	+		+		+	R-S	M to F
Yoruk	Turkey	+		+			S	C to M

Key to Chart:

Generic Name—Term used by dealer to categorize carpet. Refers to tribe, village, town, district, or country of origin.

Repeat Medallion—The same large motifs symmetrically duplicated across the main field, or two or more medallions repeated down the center of the carpet.

R—Room sized

S—Scatter sized

K—Kellegi, approximately 5 x 10 square feet and larger with length about two times the width.

I—Iran

A—Afghanistan

B—Belouchistan

C—Coarse weave—maximum of approx. 50 knots per square inch.

M—Medium weave—approx. 51 to 150 knots per square inch.

F—Fine weave—approx. 151 or more knots per square inch.

Index